Coach It Further

Patrick Sweeney, Bob Underwood, and Ron Mulson—Thank you for helping me change my circumstances and inspiring me to coach it further.

Douglas—Thank you for your unwavering support over the last 17 years.

Coach It Further

Using the Art of Coaching to Improve School Leadership

Peter M. DeWitt

Foreword by Coach Ron Mulson

CORWIN
A SAGE Publishing Company

A SAGE Publishing Company

For Information:

Corwin
A SAGE Company
2455 Teller Road
Thousand Oaks, California 91320
(800) 233-9936
www.corwin.com

SAGE Publications Ltd.
1 Oliver's Yard
55 City Road
London EC1Y 1SP
United Kingdom

SAGE Publications India Pvt. Ltd.
B 1/I 1 Mohan Cooperative Industrial Area
Mathura Road, New Delhi 110 044
India

SAGE Publications Asia-Pacific Pte. Ltd.
3 Church Street
#10-04 Samsung Hub
Singapore 049483

Publisher: Arnis Burvikovs
Development Editor: Desirée A. Bartlett
Editorial Assistant: Eliza Erickson
Production Editor: Amy Schroller
Copy Editor: Tina Hardy
Typesetter: Hurix Digital
Proofreader: Dennis W. Webb
Cover Designer: Alexa Turner
Marketing Manager: Sharon Pendergast

Copyright © 2019 by Corwin

Printed in the United States of America

Library of Congress Cataloging-in-Publication Data

Names: DeWitt, Peter M., author.

Title: Coach it further : using the art of coaching to improve school leadership / Peter M. DeWitt.

Description: Thousand Oaks, California : Corwin, 2018. | Includes bibliographical references and index.

Identifiers: LCCN 2018019949 | ISBN 9781506399492 (pbk. : alk. paper)

Subjects: LCSH: Educational leadership. | Mentoring in education. | School management and organization. | Communication in education. | School environment.

Classification: LCC LB2805 .D479 2018 | DDC 371.2—dc23

LC record available at https://lccn.loc.gov/2018019949

This book is printed on acid-free paper.

FSC
www.fsc.org
MIX
Paper from
responsible sources
FSC® C005010

18 19 20 21 22 10 9 8 7 6 5 4 3 2 1

Contents

Foreword

It was close to three decades ago when I first heard the name Pete DeWitt. I was the cross-country coach at Hudson Valley Community College (HVCC) in Troy, New York, when I learned that a talented runner from a very good high school program was interested in becoming part of our team. I had conversations with Pete about attending HVCC but in the end he decided to attend another college farther away from home. I'd like to think that I was a pretty good coach but I know that I was not a great recruiter. If I did not sincerely believe that my school was the best fit for each athlete I would happily wish them well at whichever school they decided to attend.

For whatever reason, Pete DeWitt had chosen another school and that was fine. A year later, I was again contacted by Pete. He had gone away and it had not worked out. He had then returned to his home to attend another college and it also had not been a success. He wanted to know if he could come back to HVCC. I will never forget the earnestness, close to desperation, in his voice. We began to make plans immediately.

In order to compete in college athletics, there is an academic standard for grade point average. Because of Pete's two previously unsuccessful college attempts, he was well below that standard—very well below. Though he could get into HVCC as a student, he would not be able to compete as an athlete until he raised his GPA. At the time, we were not certain if this would take a semester, a year, or a decade, but we came up with a plan. I wanted Pete to be involved with our team because I believed that this would give him the feeling of belonging that is so crucial for student motivation. I also knew that if he was not involved with the team as soon as he started classes, he could lose motivation and drift away.

The strategy was simple. He could not be on our roster and could not compete for us, but he would come to practices and participate in as many team activities as possible. There was, however, a catch. He needed to attend study skill sessions in the HVCC Learning Assistance Center a certain number of times per week. If he missed a session, the deal was off. I had used the Learning Assistance Center for years to teach study skills to my students with consistently outstanding successes. Over my teaching career I have learned that most unsuccessful students have more than enough ability to succeed but simply lack classroom and study skills. When they make mistakes, they often jump right past thinking that they need to improve those skills to assuming they don't have enough ability. By gaining simple skills, they begin to find success, and they begin to believe in themselves. This was the hope for Pete DeWitt.

Pete adjusted quickly to the new college and teammates and kept his part of the bargain. Soon he was doing well in the classroom and gaining confidence. His academic goals changed from simply surviving to excelling. The season and fall semester ended and Pete was an academic success story, not only passing his courses but making the dean's list. He returned in the spring with the same drive and focus and again thrived in the classroom. By the following fall semester, his grades had improved so dramatically that his overall GPA had risen to the point that he was eligible to compete as a member of the team. The same Pete Dewitt who had trained with and helped out the team the previous year, doing whatever task was asked of him, returned in a very different place. Those tasks as the time were not always glamorous. Whether it was timing runners, moving cones, or cleaning up after a home meet, he had done them all, and now he returned as the team captain. In an incredible season, Pete's maturity and leadership helped take a group of overachievers to a nearly top-five finish in the men's national championships and an individual victory in the women's national championships. Pete was flourishing both in and out of the classroom and upon graduation transferred to a four-year program in teacher education. He has since gone on to become a teacher, an author, and an administrator. He earned his EdD and became a highly respected principal and then educational consultant and writer.

The role of leader can be equally fulfilling and frustrating. I have often felt that leaders get too much credit when things go well and too much blame when things go poorly. Anyone who has been in a position of accountability will find a connection to this book, whether it involves feeling the weight of sole responsibility or experiencing 2 a.m. wakeup calls, which rarely solve the problems of the previous day and often have a negative effect on the ability to think clearly the following day.

This book will provide practical solutions framed by the efficacy theories of Albert Bandura. It is written by someone who has both studied and experienced the use of collaborative leadership strategies as a technique for utilizing assets and enabling success. It will also place a great deal of emphasis on the idea of working with coaches. This concept can seem counterintuitive to leaders, because as leaders, they are supposed to know all of the solutions to all of the problems themselves. I have always found it interesting that the best athletes, the greatest entertainers, and the most important world figures utilize advisors and coaches to help them perfect their skills, but educators often believe that they should be able to generate successful outcomes to every issue all by themselves. Leadership involves the use of skills. Skills are learned, not inherent, and if anyone has an appreciation for the significance of learned skills to success, it is Pete DeWitt. This book will provide a path to leadership skills for readers to put into practice as they work toward success.

It is with a great deal of pride that I have followed the development of Pete DeWitt to Peter DeWitt and later to Dr. Peter DeWitt. I would like to believe that I helped play a small role in this success, but I am realistic enough to understand that Pete had the abilities and talents all along; he just needed some guidance to find the necessary skills and then the time and space to develop them. When Dr. Peter DeWitt writes about leadership, he writes from the perspective of someone who has had an exceptionally varied combination of life experiences: the struggling student, the honors student, the teacher in both urban and rural educational settings, the administrator, the scholar, and the advocate for those who need support. He is a rare combination of theorist and pragmatist, and his insights on leadership are both thought provoking and useful. They also may help many educators get closer to that ever-elusive good night's sleep.

—*Coach Ron Mulson*

Preface

WHY WE NEED COACHES IN EDUCATIONAL LEADERSHIP

Coaching typically involves two or more people working together to help each other grow professionally and personally. Many of us think of sports when it comes up, but coaching has been a part of the educational profession for decades. What began as peer coaching in education has evolved into instructional coaching and now leadership coaching.

This book focuses on the art of coaching and how leadership coaches can work with principals. Additionally, it also dives into how principals can use the art of coaching to coach their assistant principals and interns. Everyone can benefit from coaching, and school principals need to have the coaching mindset with their assistant principals as much as a coach needs to have the mindset with the leaders they work with.

Anyone who has been in a leadership position knows that leadership is not for the faint of heart. There are so many different issues demanding leaders' time. Pont, Nusche, and Moorman (2008) indicated the following:

- More and more tasks have been added to school leaders' workload.
- Most of the school leadership tasks are carried out by one individual.
- Most school leaders receive insufficient preparation and training.

Leaders are charged with many responsibilities. Viviane Robinson (2011) noted the most important aspects of instructional leadership (listed here in order from most effective to student learning to least effective):

- Leading teacher learning and development
- Establishing goals and expectations
- Ensuring quality teaching
- Resourcing strategically
- Ensuring an orderly and safe environment (p. 9)

Unfortunately, too many leaders believe they have to be experts at every single one of these responsibilities. We need to change this way of thinking. No one person can meet all of the demands of school leadership by himself or herself. And no one needs to be an expert at everything. What leaders need is the confidence to know that they can meet their leadership responsibilities by working with their staff and school community so they can change the climate and culture of a building. Only then will they see vast improvements in student and adult learning. Self-efficacy (belief in one's capability of achieving a goal) is at the heart of how we move forward.

In this book, you will be drawn into an ongoing narrative illustrating the complexities of both leadership coaching and running a school. The narratives herein depict the real struggles of real people, not some easy scenario where everyone jumps on board at the beginning and all problems are solved with one quick conversation. We know that is not what truly happens in schools.

The book also includes K–12 student vignettes where students from North America, Australia, and Europe offer suggestions of what they want from their school leaders, their teachers, and their schools.

Stories Matter

This book is a departure from my previous books because it is essentially a narrative. Typically, I have written books on education grounded in research, which also offer practical suggestions on how to take that research and use it in the school building or classroom. With this book, I decided to take a risk and instead write a narrative involving multiple characters. I believe stories have a way of drawing us in a little deeper and help us see how ideas really do play out. The unfolding story that takes place between Michelle (a coach) and Gavin (a school principal) shows the relationship between a coach and leader. However, I wanted a real story, so I added in other characters and real-life situations that play out in our schools. These stories will hopefully make you feel as if you are in the story with Michelle and Gavin.

As you read, you will discover the evolution of the coaching relationship among Michelle, Gavin, and other characters. In many of the chapters, additional characters are highlighted to help you gain a deeper understanding of where diverse personalities and roles function in the larger narrative between Michelle and Gavin. We all have a story, and our story is the reason we approach situations from different perspectives.

AUDIENCE FOR THIS BOOK

This book is for leadership coaches who want to deepen their impact with the leaders they coach. Additionally, this book is for principals who want to use the art of coaching to have an impact on their assistant principals. And finally, this book is for principals who want to be coached, because you will find suggestions on how to move forward even if you do not have access to a full-time leadership coach.

If you are a coach who coaches principals, you will find—suggestions on how to approach principals new to coaching, ways to set goals, insights into areas of leadership that need coaching support, and the necessary components of the coaching process.

If you are a principal being coached by a leadership coach, you will find—ways to advocate for your goal, ideas that may cause you to reflect on how you receive feedback, and ways to identify particular areas that you might want to focus on as a leader.

If you are a principal who coaches assistant principals, you will find—how important it is for you to coach your assistant principal, areas where your assistant principal needs support, and suggestions on how you can build collective efficacy with your assistant principals, which will in turn help them become better leaders and help improve your leadership practice as well.

THE SELF-EFFICACY OF LEADERSHIP

As a leader, have you ever felt insecure—that level of insecurity that makes you wonder if you are cut out for the role? Then as your insecurities seem to be getting the best of you, is there a day that comes when you feel as though there is a flow to the work and you're on top of the world because everything is going well?

I, too, had my share of both good and bad days, but what seemed to always make the situation better was surrounding myself with people I could learn from and talk to about anything. Having a confidant or critical friend is important for our growth as leaders. We need people who can ask the right questions and give us insight into the issues we are facing because they have faced it before.

We all know that leadership is complex work. It involves being a manager, disciplinarian, instructional guide, and collaborative motivator. For school leaders to have a real impact on student learning, they need to collaborate with many different stakeholders in order to change the climate and culture of a building. To me, *climate* is how students, staff, and families feel when they walk into a school building. Do they see images on the walls that are representative of the school's student population? Do they feel like members of the school community, or do school staff make them feel as though they are visitors within their own school?

Culture is a bit different and is something that happens over the long term. Culture is what happens after teachers and leaders have been there for a while. This means, in a positive culture, people work hard to meet the needs of students and empower them so their student voice feels valued. A negative culture is one that has low expectations of students, and year after year students enter into the school knowing teachers, staff, and leaders think less of them.

We need positive school climates and cultures where voices feel valued. Gone should be the days when leaders handpicked only yes-men and women for stakeholder groups. In order to be optimally effective, we must collaborate with people who challenge our thinking.

Leadership self-efficacy (LSE) is about principals understanding themselves as leaders and then figuring out how they (as coaches) can help teachers and school staff develop their own leadership skills. School cultures where the

Figure I.1   Effects of Leadership Self-Efficacy in a School

LSE Present	LSE Not Present
Colleagues are committed to collective capacity.	Colleagues follow individual pursuits.
Staff are more persistent in pursuing goals together.	Staff quickly give up on goals.
Staff are more confident when they choose to take risks in the classroom.	Individuals are more insecure of their choice to try new approaches in the classroom.
Staff are collectively more proactive in preventing problems.	Individuals are more reactive when problems arise.
Staff report greater job satisfaction.	Staff display burnout in larger numbers.
A motivating culture is present and felt.	Staff find the culture of the school to be debilitating.
Staff experience a common moral purpose.	Staff display a lack of commitment.

Adapted from Leithwood and Jantzi (2008).

principal functions as both a leadership coach to others and a strong collaborative leader have seen significant benefits in attaining common goals, working effectively together as a team, and promoting a climate that is welcoming and nurturing to all. LSE plus collaborative leadership lead to collective self-efficacy where, together, the school staff work as an effective team and are therefore far more effective in improving student learning overall (see Figure I.1).

LEADERSHIP SHOULDN'T BE A SOLITARY PURSUIT

We work better when we learn collectively with others. That collective work provides us with people to have deep conversations with, and they challenge our thinking around the topic we are working on. Good leaders inspire people to authentically work together through challenging each other around a problem of practice in order to improve their educational surroundings. Getting people to work together is part of collective efficacy, which is the extension of self-efficacy.

Coaching leaders is a way to help them grow in their leadership practices, which will benefit everyone in the school community. That is why I believe that principals should be encouraged, and given the autonomy, to coach their assistant principals. It's a win-win for everyone and will help build capacity in a school community.

Coaching doesn't necessarily mean that school districts have to bring in coaches from an outside agency. Sometimes coaching happens when two leaders work together in a critical friendship. In some districts, the superintendent or assistant superintendent works on a goal with a principal and they go through a coaching cycle together. In some small districts (in the United States) or school boards (in Canada), district leadership has the capacity to coach building leaders. Likewise, in some large districts or school boards, regional superintendents and assistant superintendents have the capacity to coach principals. Unfortunately, some districts and school boards do not have the capacity for these types of coaching relationships. In these districts, it might be a good option to explore hiring coaches from outside the district or pairing up principals with each other to work as peer coaches or mentor coaches where more experienced principals mentor newer principals.

All principals, whether veterans or novices, can benefit from working on a goal with a leadership coach. Furthermore, all principals can guide and mentor their own staff by serving as coaches to assistant principals and aspiring teacher leaders. Coaching happens when two people work together around a goal and look for improvement in the impact they are having on those around them, including students, teachers, and families (see Figure I.2).

Coaches need to understand self-efficacy if they are to help people meet their maximum potential. Simply being in a position of leadership doesn't mean those individuals have

Figure I.2   Four Types of Coaching Relationships in Education

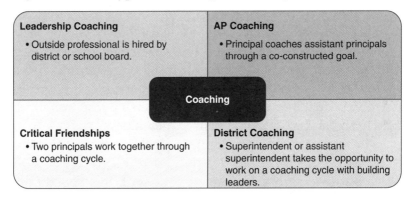

Leadership Coaching	AP Coaching
• Outside professional is hired by district or school board.	• Principal coaches assistant principals through a co-constructed goal.
Coaching	
Critical Friendships	District Coaching
• Two principals work together through a coaching cycle.	• Superintendent or assistant superintendent takes the opportunity to work on a coaching cycle with building leaders.

Coach's Corner

Virtual Coaching

Leaders in small districts often work with coaches via Twitter, Voxer, Skype, or other online tools. Distant coaches may not be able to travel to the location of the principal, but they can act as a sounding board for leaders, helping to guide them through a problem or practice. I believe the jury is still out where

(Continued)

(Continued)

virtual coaching is concerned because I wonder if you can ever have an authentic conversation about impact if the two parties never meet.

- How do we know the leaders do what they say they do?
- Where is the evidence of impact?

the skills to help those around them improve. Likewise, being leaders doesn't mean they know how to improve or know what to improve upon. Some leaders only focus on what to fix outward and never spend enough time looking inward to see what needs fixing first.

School leaders are often so busy that they do not have the time or presence of mind to examine the merits of the goals they are currently pursuing or how they can improve their current strategies to have a deeper impact in achieving their current goals. They also often neglect to take the time to understand their skill set, and they rarely get feedback that focuses on their self-efficacy as a leader. This is where coaching comes in. Committing to a period of coaching for a set length of time helps leaders work toward a goal and hone particular leadership practices so that they can tackle their leadership responsibilities with fresh perspectives and renewed motivation.

Whether you are a seasoned coach, a leader looking to be coached, or a leader looking for guidance on how to coach burgeoning leaders among your staff, this book offers insights, reflection questions, tips, and much more.

Special Features

In this book you will find the following:

- **More authentic stories, less educational rhetoric**—This book is different because it shares exchanges between people, much like Patrick Lencioni did in his 2005 book, *Overcoming the Five Dysfunctions of a Team.*

- **The collaborative leadership growth cycle**—The goal of this graphic is to provide leaders with a starting point and offer them very specific steps to take to reach their goal.
- **Four priorities**—Research has revealed four priorities that school leaders are most concerned about. This book offers practical strategies supported by research to help school leaders meet those four priorities. The priorities are collective efficacy, communication, student and community engagement, and the political climate.
- **Stories from the field**—Interwoven in the ongoing narrative are real vignettes from leaders and students.
- **"Coach's Corner"**—Throughout the book there are several practical suggestions on how you can move forward in your coaching and leadership practice.
- **Discussion questions**—At the end of each chapter you will find actionable questions for leadership coaches to use with their leader-coachees.

IN THE END

This book is about understanding our impact. It is about raising our own leadership self-efficacy and helping to raise it in others. Leadership coaching can be one way to help leaders hone in on a goal that will be both personally and professionally impactful.

The mindsets of the coach and the person being coached are critical factors in the success of the coaching endeavor. Both parties have to want to be engaged in the process. In the following chapters, readers will read the fictional story of new school leader Gavin and his leadership coach Michelle. Their story will provide insights as to how coaching can work. While the story is not autobiographical, some of the issues experienced by Gavin and Michelle are those I went through as a principal.

Coaching is about fostering a confidential relationship between coach and leader, where they learn from one another and focus solely on the decisions they come to together, rather than goals imposed from others. It is imperative that district leaders invest in principals and aspiring principals. This means providing leaders with the support they need to develop self-efficacy and improve their practice as collaborative leaders.

Acknowledgments

I have been very fortunate to meet many people over the last year while writing this book, as well as receive constant support from my family. They have all helped bring collaborative leadership work to the next level, and I would like to thank them.

My family—I couldn't do it without you. Everyone should be as fortunate to have a family like you.

Peter Slattery and Peter Mesh—You make everyone around you better.

Jim Verlengia—Thank you for all of your hard work and support in bringing collaborative leadership work to the state level in Iowa. I really enjoy working with good-hearted people, and you are among the best.

Lisa Pryor, Robin Anderson, Jennifer Cutler, Linda Everett, Charlotte Jones, Kathy Taber, and Jaycie Smith— Thank you for your deep coaching in Cohort 2.

Cohort 2 of MovingUP—It was an honor to work with you.

Dave Ksanznak—Thanks for being the best cooperating teacher, coach, and mentor a student teacher could ever ask for.

Ardith Shirley, Jill Ott, Linda Massey, and Jan Murphy—Thank you for bringing the work to the New Brunswick Teachers' Association and principals, as well as the Ontario Principals' Council.

Matt, Teri, Christina, Libby, Kim, and Eric—Thanks for allowing me to be your coach.

Amanda Kavanagh, Billy Krakower, Danielle Gately, LaQuita Outlaw, David Casamento, Dennis Schug, Donald Gately, Ed Kemnitzer, and Erin Marone—Thanks for engaging in School Climate as a book club. I loved learning from all of you.

John Hattie, Jim Knight, and Andy Hargreaves—Thank you for your support over the years. It is amazing to know, and work with, all of you.

Collaborative Leadership Group: Jenni Donohoo, Kara Vandas, Tommy Thompson, Jon Krownapple, Erin Clark Krownapple, Nicole Franks, Sonja Alexander, and Ken Lein—I am looking forward to building capacity with all of you.

Michelle Hebert—Thank you for giving me my first break into educational writing.

Elizabeth Rich and Kathleen Manzo—Writing for *Education Week* changed my life. Thank you for that.

Arnis Burvikovs, Desiree Bartlett, and Eliza Erickson—Your editing makes me a better writer … I hope!

Publisher's Acknowledgments

Corwin gratefully acknowledges the contributions of the following reviewers:

Angela Becton
Director of Advanced Learning
Smithfield, NC

Ray Boyd
Principal
Beechboro, Western Australia

Ken Darvall
Principal
Tema, Ghana

Jessica Johnson
Principal, District Assessment Coordinator
Juneau, WI

Jacie Maslyk
Assistant Superintendent
Aliquippa, PA

About the Author

Peter M. DeWitt, EdD, is a former K–5 teacher (11 years) and principal (8 years). He runs workshops and provides keynotes nationally and internationally, focusing on collaborative leadership and fostering inclusive school climates. Within North America, his work has been adopted at the university and state level, and he works with numerous districts, school boards, and regional and state organizations, where he trains leadership teams and coaches building leaders.

Additionally, Peter is a Visible Learning trainer for John Hattie and was an instructional coach for Jim Knight for several years. He is the series editor for the Connected Educator Series and the Impact Leadership Series (Corwin), which include books by Viviane Robinson, Pasi Sahlberg, Yong Zhao, and Michael Fullan.

His *Finding Common Ground* blog (http://blogs.edweek .org/edweek/finding_common_ground/) has been published by *Education Week* since 2011. He is the 2013 School Administrators Association of New York State's (SAANYS) Outstanding Educator of the Year and the 2015 Education Blogger of the Year (Academy of Education Arts & Sciences).

Peter is the author of several books, including *Collaborative Leadership: Six Influences That Matter Most* (Corwin/Learning

Forward, 2016) and *School Climate: Leading With Collective Efficacy* (Corwin/Ontario Principals' Council, 2017).

His articles have appeared in education journals at the state, national, and international level, and he has presented at forums, conferences, and panel discussions at all three levels as well. Highlights include presenting for the National Association of Elementary School Principals (NAESP), ASCD, and NBC's *Education Nation.*

1

BEGINNING A COACHING RELATIONSHIP

We know that coaching can be helpful to our growth. Often, leaders are fully on board with teachers working with coaches. However, as leaders, we sometimes feel as though we are not successful in our job if our superintendent suggests we work with a coach. We often put pressure on ourselves to know everything. We think to ourselves, "What will the staff think of me if they know I'm working with a coach?" Or, "Will I lose credibility with staff when they find out I am working with a coach?" Our insecurities can get the best of us sometimes.

Where this is a little different is when a principal uses the coaching mindset with his or her assistant principals. It's easier to digest because assistant principals expect constant evaluative feedback from their principals. It is a missed opportunity that many principals do not apply a coaching mindset in their relationship with their assistant principals. Perhaps the situation that plays out in the following chapters will help principals understand how they can coach it further with growing leaders on their staff.

In this chapter you will meet Gavin, a new principal. His story and his insecurities may not be unlike yours.

//

Introducing: Gavin, Beth, Brad, and Dr. Coppola

Principal: Gavin Young

Assistant Principals: Beth Lopez and Brad Washington

Superintendent: Dr. Mayan Coppola

//

Gavin Young is a first-year principal at Naylor Middle School, which is a suburban school district charged with educating 754 students. Approximately 61% of the student population is White, 27% is African American, 5% is Latino, 3% is Asian, and 4% identifies as Native American/Indigenous. Approximately 18% of the students qualify for special education. Additionally, school staff are beginning to see an increase in the students who identify as gay or lesbian and some who identify as transgender. All of this has an impact on the school climate (how students, staff, and parents feel on campus).

Besides approximately 62 teachers, there are 37 support staff, or what some schools refer to as classified staff. Gavin also has two assistant principals, Beth Lopez and Brad Washington, on his team. Sadly, team is a loose interpretation of how they function. Although Beth is very supportive of Gavin's leadership, as she has known him for over a decade because she was a school counselor in his former school district, Brad is another story. Brad has been an assistant principal with the district for five years, and to make matters more complicated, he interviewed for the job that Gavin now has. The reason he was passed over is that he isn't exactly a ball of fire. He plays a more passive role in the building, but he went for the job because of higher pay and more status.

Although many of the teachers in the building were not surprised that Brad didn't get the job, it certainly was a surprise to Brad, who assumed he was a shoo-in, and he hasn't quite warmed up to the idea that he is still the assistant principal.

Although Gavin had been an assistant principal for three years in a neighboring school district, he doesn't always feel confident as a school principal, but given that he only has 50% support on his leadership team, he isn't ready to admit that to either Beth or Brad. He worries that Brad will see it as a weakness and use it, and he doesn't want to confide in Beth because he doesn't want to put her in the middle.

Gavin lacks a belief in his own capabilities when it comes to leadership, but it isn't on his radar to a deep extent. He figures it's just part of being new in the job. He sometimes wishes he felt more prepared, but he believes that if he just keeps plugging along, he will be fine.

WHAT TO DO VERSUS WHAT NOT TO DO

Gavin's previous administrative experience leading up to his head principalship wasn't helpful either. Most of his days as an assistant principal were spent focusing on task completion or tasks that his supervising principal didn't want to do. He didn't have a lot of time for relationship building, and when he was seen talking with teachers the principal didn't like, he was often asked what they were discussing.

Gavin spent most of his time with discipline issues and was not able to visit as many classrooms as he wanted to, which created a disconnection with staff. He felt as though his principal used him as a gopher, which meant "go for this" and "go for that." His previous experience could be categorized as more of a case of what not to do rather than what to do in leadership. Unfortunately, due to his training and his experiences thus far as a school leader, what not to do is not always as obvious to Gavin. He simply doesn't always know what he doesn't know.

Gavin's actions reveal that he believes leadership is more management than focusing on instructional impact and learning, despite what the books and blogs say. He is good at maintaining schedules and checking the halls for behavior issues, but he is nervous about entering classrooms. What Gavin doesn't understand is that his resistance to entering classrooms ultimately will hurt his credibility when trying to give feedback to his teachers who will not trust his assessments if they never see him observing their classes. Additionally, he lacks the knowledge that there are multiple ways to lead, and his former supervisor was less coach and more dictator, so the coaching mindset didn't exist. And he now finds himself on a team where one person is supportive and the other is judging his every move.

Gavin worked hard in his administrative training courses at the university level, but he often felt a divide between what he learned in class and what he was asked to do in his role as assistant principal.

Coach's Corner

Strategies for Coaching Assistant Principals

As a principal, do you have an assistant principal or several of them? Do you coach them or are they left to their own devices? Although you may have hired qualified leaders as assistants, they still need some coaching. If they are only allowed to handle discipline, which was the case in Gavin's previous position, they may move forward knowing only how to deal with that one area. Leaders in the making need more than that. As a principal, you should do the following:

- Spend time focusing on instructional leadership strategies with your assistant principals.
- Teach them how to foster relationships with staff.
- Coach them to work toward having more dialogue in their meetings with stakeholders. We do this by offering questions they can ask and having dialogue in our meetings with them.
- Lead by example.

AM I IN OVER MY HEAD?

Truthfully, getting the job at Naylor Middle School seemed to be the easy part. Over the summer months, Gavin spent a lot of time getting ready for the school year, and he was fairly engaged at the district administration meetings. But let's face it—it's easier to be engaged when students and teachers are not yet present in school. His insecurities started to come to light when he spent more time with Brad. He worried Brad would judge what he said or interrupt and have a contrary opinion to the one Gavin had.

It was when the school year began that he worried he was in over his head, but he was too stubborn to admit it and too insecure to do much about it. Self-efficacy is situation specific, and he began having a hard time finding out where he excelled and where he needed growth. Most times he felt as though he only had areas of growth and no areas of expertise. However, every day he put his head down and walked into the building, and due to his insecurities, he began demanding compliance through some of his rules and regulations.

It didn't help that he was dealing with a lawsuit from parents that stemmed from a lack of special education services for their child the year before, and he was getting pushback from a few teachers and parents for creating a "gender-neutral" bathroom for several students identifying as transgender. Even though the director of special education was working through the lawsuit, and state law supported the creation of the gender-neutral bathroom, both situations were sources of stress for Gavin.

Gavin began to see that his insecurities were getting in the way of establishing a supportive school climate for students, parents, and teachers. There were times he chalked it up to cultural issues the school district always had or an unresponsive school superintendent when he went to her with his issues. He felt that these issues that were created by his predecessor were getting in the way of his chance to be the leader he wanted to be, so he would just be the leader that he learned from in his previous experience. Gavin was feeling a constant push and pull. No leadership position is easy from the start, and this one had a great deal of potential. But Gavin was finding himself becoming angry on the job.

Coach's Corner

Strategies for Addressing Insecurities

Every leader goes through moments of insecurity. Bad leadership happens when we don't do anything about it. What can insecure leaders do when they feel insecure?

- Seek the help of a coach.
- Find a confidant (i.e., friend, colleague, partner, spouse, etc.).
- Be honest with yourself about the insecurities.
- Join a professional learning community in your region or on social media.
- Understand that you are not alone.

Like any new leader, Gavin's sleeping patterns were affected. He found himself waking up in the middle of the night and worrying about things that may or may not ever happen. When his alarm went off at 5 a.m., Gavin was tired, and this was beginning to affect how he interacted with staff and students. He hoped this was somewhat temporary, but it was beginning to get to him. He started spending a great deal of time on the managerial side. Like any new leader he was reactive, and he wondered if he would ever reach the point of becoming proactive.

Gavin knew that good leadership begins with relationships. In John Hattie's research (e.g., Hattie 2012a, 2012b), which involves over 300 million students, teacher–student relationships have an effect size of .72, which is well over the hinge point of .40, which equates to a year's worth of growth for a year's input. Relationships among the adults in school are equally important because they are at the heart of creating a supportive school climate.

Due to his feeling of being in over his head, combined with the need for relationships, Gavin joined social media and began creating a professional learning community (PLC) using Twitter and Facebook. Additionally, he joined a small group of middle school principals via Voxer. These principals were all within their first three years of leadership. They talked a great deal about their experiences, and the conversations always came back to relationships. But Gavin felt like the people in the Voxer group were being much more proactive in their schools than he was, and he felt as though the other principals had much stronger teams. His insecurities began to grow and get the best of him, and he found less time to interact with the principal group.

Coach's Corner

Leadership PLCs on Voxer

- Voxer is a walkie-talkie app that can be downloaded to your smartphone.
- Users can create groups of two or more and leave messages for those in the group.
- Voxer will automatically ask if you want to import your Facebook, email, and Twitter contacts.
- Search the Voxer database for school leadership groups.
- Join the Voxer group of your choice and begin a conversation.
- Voxer is a way to create a PLC with colleagues near and far.

Gavin knew that if he wanted his teachers to build strong relationships with students because of its high effect size, he needed to build strong relationships with teachers first. Whether that was welcoming them in the main office every morning or talking with them in the hallway every day, Gavin was making a concerted effort to be the first person at school, and he was going to try his best to have face-to-face conversations with as many teachers as he could, as often as possible. Unfortunately, he didn't always know whether these methods were working, mostly because he did most of the talking, and the teachers were in a hurry to get out of his office.

As Gavin worked to foster relationships with staff, he also began working hard to get to know students. He would often invite groups into his office and ask them what they wanted out of their principal, or he would use the morning announcements to invite students to write him letters of advice. He got the idea from some principals in his professional learning network (PLN). As an example of how it can look, one of his PLN members sent him the following vignette written by a sophomore.

An Ideal Principal Should . . .

If we want to build relationships with all stakeholders, we need to listen to what the students say. The following is insight given by Ainsley, a 10th grader from Albany, New York.

An ideal principal should listen to students, be involved, reasonable, approachable, supportive and willing to make a change for the school. A principal should attend school events like plays, games, and competitions to show support for the hard work of their students. They should be more aware and involved with club success and happiness.

When a whole club is unhappy about how it is being run and they have tried everything to make a change themselves, a principal should listen to those kids and make the needed change so they can enjoy the club and pursue their interests.

Most importantly, a principal should smile more, get to know students' names to create an approachable relationship, and create a friendly atmosphere. Students should be able to rely on a principal to be their voice when no one will listen. A principal shouldn't be so intimidating that students are too fearful to look at them.

A principal should treat all students equally no matter their race, gender, body shape, and mental state. A principal shouldn't make a girl feel like a distraction for wearing a shirt that shows her shoulders but allow a boy to walk through the halls with a muscle tank. Instead of worrying about a tank top strap being two fingers wide, a principal should be worrying about the safety of the students and staff.

A principal needs to make sure that all teachers understand and take safety drills like lockdowns and fire drills seriously so in the event of an actual emergency the staff can be trusted with the lives of the students. They should approach a teacher if multiple students file complaints of harassment or bullying. A principal should also award students for their academic, athletic, or theatrical excellence, and make sure that all students and staff are safe at all times.

Principal Sophie Murphy from Melbourne, Australia, also sent Gavin a few vignettes that offered advice for principals. This is from Poppy, a 12-year-old student.

> *A principal should know who you are, they don't need to know EVERY-*
> *THING that you do, but a student should be able to talk to their princi-*
> *pal and tell them something that they have achieved. Another quality*
> *that all principals should have is that they should be kind of involved*
> *with the students at school and they should know what is going with*
> *the students.*
>
> *We like to see our principal in our class and outside at the beginning or*
> *end of the day. I think that a good principal should not only know your*
> *name (very important) but know who you are, and sometimes give you*
> *a secret wink, especially on days where you need that—a good Principal*
> *knows when to give you that smile or wink!*

Gavin smiled when he read the words of advice and was glad that he began talking with students about school and leadership. His leadership wasn't perfect, especially with some of the adults in the building, but he often felt inspired by his conversations with students, and he knew that he could use their insight. At times Brad scoffed at Gavin's need to interview students in focus groups, but Beth often came to his defense and said how important it was to foster student voice.

IT'S TIME FOR A COACH

As hard as Gavin tried to establish relationships with teachers, parents, and students, he was met with resistance. Gavin's predecessor at Naylor Middle School had not been known for his instructional, nor collaborative, leadership. From the stories he was told, Gavin's predecessor at Naylor had the very same mindset as his former supervising principal. In actuality, his predecessor was known for having his favorite teachers, which were typically the ones who made his life easy, and he was a bit more of a compliance-based principal when it came to those teachers who questioned his motives or leadership. Due to his insecurities, Gavin found it easier to blame his predecessor than look within and try to change the circumstances created for him. He was tired of not achieving the level of success he wanted.

Although he didn't always feel that he was supported by his superintendent, she was in fact a helpful presence in the school community. When we are in the depths of despair as a leader, it's easy to blame everyone around us and not see how they are really trying to help us, especially if they give us feedback we don't want to hear.

Superintendent Dr. Mayan Coppola knew that Gavin had a great deal of potential and she believed in him, but she felt he needed some assistance to understand his strengths and weaknesses. She knew that the school staff lacked cohesiveness because of the previous leader, and she was worried that without definitive change in the school culture and practices, that lack of cohesiveness would continue. She also understood that Brad was a challenge to the team. She had given Gavin a heads-up that Brad interviewed for the job, because she didn't want to blindside him, but she also knew that part of being the school leader is dealing with the internal jealousies of the staff. Although school leadership is supposed to be all about the students, too often it's all about the adults.

Dr. Coppola was experienced enough to understand that insecurities as a leader can create a pretty corrosive school climate, and she saw the warning signs that Gavin was going down that road. However, from the moment she met him at the interview for the principalship, she felt that he had something positive to offer, and she intended to help him find it. Dr. Coppola told Gavin she thought he would benefit from working with a coach. She had been a principal for six years before becoming superintendent, and as much as she loved it, she also knew the obstacles Gavin faced. What Gavin didn't always realize was that Dr. Coppola did not look for perfection as much as she focused on Gavin's potential.

Dr. Coppola managed a large district, so she would not be able to check on Gavin every day, nor did she want to. Her goal was to build his leadership capacity, so she enlisted a coach for him. When she went to Naylor Middle School for a visit, she sat with Gavin and told him she remembered what it was like to be new in a position of leadership and that she loved that he had a desire to be more proactive and place a bigger focus on learning.

Dr. Coppola told Gavin that she wanted him to reach his full potential and felt that coaching was the way to do it. There were some other principals working with a coach in the district, and she thought it would be a good fit for Gavin as well. He wondered if Brad would be working with a coach, because he needed it more, but Gavin decided not to bring that up in the conversation with Dr. Coppola.

Dr. Coppola had some ground rules. She wanted Gavin and the coach's relationship to be confidential. All she asked was to be kept abreast of the growth that Gavin and his new coach would be tracking. Additionally, the coaching relationship would only take place over the year, because coach's job was to build capacity with Gavin so he could then build it with staff. Leadership coaching is not supposed to be a lifetime crutch. Gavin's body language showed Dr. Coppola that he was both more insecure than when she entered his office and that he was resistant to having a coach.

Sensing his reluctance, Dr. Coppola gave Gavin a few days to think it over. Initially, Gavin wasn't on board with the idea. His insecurities about Brad were clouding his judgement. He felt that although his inexperience contributed to the problem, significant issues affecting his school were bigger than those a coach could handle. Still, he understood that the suggestion of a coach was more of a requirement than an option and given that, he planned to make the most out of the coaching relationship.

Feeling insecure and needing to confide in someone outside of the district, Gavin emailed his cousin, Ardith Shirley, a member of the New Brunswick Teachers' Association in Canada, for advice. Within a few hours, Ardith responded.

Hi Gavin,

When the term 'coach' is used, many people first connect to memories of a hockey, football, or other athletic coach from their past. Others will assume a more hierarchical relationship often associated with that of a mentor and mentee. Depending on personal experiences in both of those contexts, news that a person has an opportunity to be coached may be met with excitement and anticipation or angst and trepidation. For this reason, it becomes very important to clarify exactly what type of coaching experience is to be expected by leaders if the goal is to improve their perceived self-efficacy. Have you had that conversation with your superintendent?

It is important to clarify that like the horse drawn 'coaches' in days of yore, the kind of 'coach' we should propose is one that assists you to get from where you are now, to where you want to be, based on your own goals, insight and wisdom. These coaching conversations are grounded in the belief that the role of coach is to support you (the leader/coachee) in finding your inner wisdom. It is not to impose external agendas or wisdom based on previous experience or expertise a coach may possess.

Gavin, I believe this is a really good idea if you feel like the coach has credibility. We all could use a coach!

Hope that helps.

Ardith

Gavin felt a bit better after reading Ardith's letter. He wanted to take some time to think all of this over, but in the end, he realized that his superintendent recommended he work with a coach, so this was less about volunteering and more about being "voluntold."

Before he turned off his computer he received an email from Dr. Coppola. He sat back a bit, feeling a bit deflated. He clicked to open up the email.

Hi Gavin,

Listen, I understand that you may be feeling a bit insecure because I offered up the idea of working with a coach. I came across this blog from *Finding Common Ground* (*Education Week*) and it helps explain where I am coming from when I suggested it.

Like I said, think it over.

Gavin clicked on the link to the blog.

Gavin finished reading the blog post and took a deep breath. He still wasn't convinced.

If Coaching Is So Powerful, Why Aren't Principals Being Coached?

blogs.edweek.org
October 16, 2016
by Peter DeWitt

If instructional coaching is beneficial to teachers, shouldn't leadership coaching be beneficial to principals?

In most instructional coaching philosophies the teacher wants to be coached. Instructional coaching expert Jim Knight, someone I work with as an instructional coaching trainer, says that teachers should be the ones to choose to enroll with the coach. Furthermore, teachers should be able to choose the goal they will work on. This initial aspect to the coaching cycle takes a lot of dialogue to get to the heart of why the goal is the best goal for them.

(Continued)

(Continued)

In those cases where a teacher doesn't know what goal to choose, but wants to do a full instructional coaching cycle, the teacher and coach co-construct the goals together. This may take a baseline observation or a teacher video-taping themselves to look at whether their engagement is authentic or compliant.

According to Knight's research, coaching is an effective way to provide individualized professional development to teachers because those teachers who choose to be a part of the coaching program are an eager participant in the process. Coaching will help teachers retain up to 90% of what they learned, as opposed to lose 90% when they go to the typical sit-and-get professional development. Knight's research certainly fits into the research of others who have studied professional development.

For example, Timperley et al. (2007) found that the most effective professional development had the following elements.

- *Over a long period of time (three to five years)*
- *Involves external experts*
- *Teachers are deeply engaged*
- *It challenges teachers' existing beliefs*
- *Teachers talk to each other about teaching*
- *School leadership supports teachers' opportunities to learn and provides opportunities within the school structure for this to happen*

Leadership support can happen in different ways. In the best-case scenario involving school leadership and teachers, a principal would suggest coaching as a way to help any teacher improve. That means teachers who may have a low level of self-efficacy (Bandura) and need assistance or a teacher who is a high flyer and can benefit from a keen eye and effective feedback.

What about principals?

If principals believe that teachers can benefit from high quality coaching, doesn't that mean that principals can as well? I wonder how many would engage in that type of professional development? Many times the school leader believes that they are supposed to know it all, which is quite possibly why they moved to the principalship. And some principals may believe coaching is for teaching and not for them, which is an interesting dilemma when it comes to who values coaching and why. If coaches are good for teachers, shouldn't coaching be valuable for leaders too?

There are leaders who believe that coaching can be just as important for them as it is for teachers. This is the collaborative, growth and innovative mindset leaders should have. If leaders truly believe in being collaborative, they also understand that they have a blind spot (Scharmer) which they lead from on a daily basis, and they may need outside guidance on how to get through that blind spot. For example, a possible blind spot is that they may enter into a situation with a confirmation bias that prevents them from seeing what is really happening in the classroom.

Let's use this scenario:

A principal may enter into a classroom of a teacher that they don't necessarily believe is a strong teacher and look for the reasons to support their bias. A coach could help principals understand that they have a bias because that coach is entering without the same confirmation bias.

Additionally, leadership coaches may help leaders understand how they can communicate better with staff, students and parents. They can even help leaders understand how to build collective efficacy.

Practice what we preach?

Coaching can be very beneficial. I've seen the benefits more now than I ever did as a principal because I have had the luxury to work with highly effective coaches around the country. They don't want the position for status or power, but they do want to coach because they have a goal of helping their peers (build collective efficacy) at the same time they learn from those peers they work with.

The same can be done at the leadership level. Building synergy among leaders and getting them to try new strategies to build collective efficacy among their staff is something coaches can help do, and they often offer an outside perspective because they have worked with many other leaders.

We know from Knight's research and the research of others including Timperley that professional development, and that's what coaching is, is a lot stronger when both parties want to be a part of it. If coaching is beneficial to teachers, we can make it better for leaders as well. We just have to have the proper collaborative, growth and innovative mindset to get there.

In the End

In this chapter, you met Gavin and learned his story. To some of you, his story might not be complicated at all and others might find that Gavin's story doesn't particularly resonate with your own. However, the insecurities that Gavin feels are ubiquitous among most leaders.

If you are a principal reading this, my hope is that you feel as though your role is part supervisor and part coach with those you lead. The coaching mindset is all about helping those around us improve in their practice. John Hattie, whom I have worked with for a number of years, always asks, "What's your impact?" Our impact is to always help others become better in their role.

In later chapters you will be introduced to Gavin's coach, Michelle Hebert. I'm not giving away the story by telling you that Gavin will work with Michelle. Let's face it, as soon as Dr. Coppola suggested working with a coach, we all knew Gavin would be working with one. However, because of Gavin's trepidation in working with a coach, there are some trials and tribulations that Gavin and Michelle will have to navigate together.

DISCUSSION QUESTIONS

Coaches and Leaders:

- What do you believe is Gavin's biggest challenge?
- If you received student letters, like those included in this chapter, how would you respond?

Leaders:

- What would you want out of a coaching experience?
- What do you want out of your leadership?
- How do you evaluate your own impact at the same time you evaluate the impact of teachers?

Coaches:

- How would you begin working with Gavin?

TAKE ACTION

- Make a list of those duties you feel most confident in doing. This helps build confidence.
  - Collect evidence that demonstrates whether you are truly successful in those areas.
  - For example, if you believe you are a good listener, videotape (with permission) a series of postobservation conversations between yourself and a teacher to see if you listen as effectively as you think you do.
- Additionally, make a list of what makes you feel insecure. We all have areas of growth. Which one stands out the most to you?
- Find a coach, colleague, or member of your PLN who will help you work on an area of growth. Partner with that individual and help him or her in an area of growth as well.
- Solicit feedback from the students in your school either through video interviews, student focus groups, an anonymous suggestion box, or letters to the editor for the school paper or newsletter.

2

GAVIN "ACCEPTS" COACHING

Coaching Credibility

In my experience in leadership coaching, superintendents and assistant superintendents contact me because they want some of their principals to be coached. There are times when the principals are new to the position and other times when they are seasoned and coaching seems like a good fit because of a challenge those principals are facing. Many conversations with the district leaders begin the same way. I am told that the principals really want to be coached and are excited about the idea of working with a coach over a year. When I agree to coaching the principals, I am assured once again that the principals are looking forward to working with me. And then I meet the principals.

It is clear from their body language that they are not overly thrilled about working with me. They agreed to it because, like Gavin, they feel as though it is a voluntold situation, or they did not realize it would be on a one-on-one basis. A common misperception is that a team of principals will be meeting with a coach as a group. When this happens, the onus is on me to help engage them. They need to know that I am there to part-ner with them and work on a goal that *they* care about.

My many years as a principal affords me some credibility, but serving time is not enough. One issue that can appear as a deficit is that I have had elementary school experience but not middle or high school. What does afford me increasing cred-ibility is my growing knowledge of what it means to be a school leader and my mounting experiences working with building and district leaders over long periods of time as well as my own expertise as a collaborative leader. As coaches or principals coaching our assistants, listening is key to the process. Those we coach have to know that we are listening to their needs, under-standing their context, and providing actionable steps that will allow them to see improvement in weeks rather than months.

One of the ways I connect with people I will coach is through the use of a preengagement survey. I use preengage-ment surveys when I run workshops because the answers I receive help me understand the contexts of those with whom I will be working. Asking about their experiences and needs also helps those I will work with see that I care about their voice and challenges. Typically, the surveys include only four items:

- What do you know about collaboration?
- Describe some of the ways in which you collaborate.
- What are you hoping to learn?
- What do you want me to know about you?

In this chapter, you will meet Michelle Hebert and learn how she approaches Gavin and works through his insecurities with him. You will also notice some pieces crucial to coaching, like a preengagement survey and a series of questions that can be used during the coaching process.

INTRODUCING LEADERSHIP COACH MICHELLE HEBERT

Gavin called Dr. Coppola after about 24 hours, few of which involved sleeping. He tossed and turned during the night, feeling insecure about his leadership, but he told Dr. Coppola that he would be willing to work with a coach. It was easier for him to lie on the phone than in person because his body language couldn't give him away. A few days later, Dr. Coppola introduced Gavin to Michelle Hebert, a retired principal and leadership coach. Michelle had an excellent reputation, and Gavin had come across her a few times when he was an assistant principal.

Michelle knew her first meeting with Gavin was going to be very important. As they say, you never get a second chance to make a first impression. Michelle assumed that Gavin had asked to work with a coach, but she soon found out that was not the case.

Coach's Corner

Credibility Matters

One of the most important qualities of a leadership coach is credibility. Leadership coaches are credible when they

- Have experience in the position they are coaching (for example, a former principal coaching current principals).
- Listen to the needs of the leader they are coaching.
- Follow through on what they say they are going to do.
- Provide resources to help the leader build capacity.
- Offer effective feedback.
- Focus on growth and short-term wins for long-term gains.

OF COURSE I WANT TO BE COACHED!

Michelle's first goal was to foster a relationship with Gavin. After she received the call from Dr. Coppola, she called Gavin to say hello. Although she made a few attempts, Gavin did not return her calls. This lack of response does not happen often to Michelle, so she knew that he was probably not as eager to be coached as she was led to believe. Michelle decided to send him an email.

Hi Gavin,

I hope this finds you well.

I am really looking forward to working and learning with you in this coaching experience. Dr. Coppola speaks very highly of you.

I know you are really busy, but I was hoping you could click on the link below to a Survey Monkey I created, and fill it out. I'd really like to get to know you a bit better before our initial meeting.

If you need anything, please feel free to call or e-mail me.

Thanks for your time.

Michelle Hebert, EdD

Gavin told himself he did not return Michelle's calls because he was busy doing other things, but in reality, he was avoiding her. Several times he obsessed a bit on the line that said, "Dr. Coppola thinks highly of you." "I bet," he thought to himself.

He decided to plunge in and take the survey. One night at home he clicked on the preengagement survey because he realized that one way or another, he had to work with Michelle. The preengagement survey was short, and he started to fill it out.

What do you hope to get out of the coaching experience?

What is one thing you would like me to know about you?

What is something you think I could learn from you?

What is the biggest challenge you face as a leader?

Gavin had the answers he wanted to give, and the answers he knew he should give. After all, he was unclear on whether this was going to truly be as confidential as he was led to believe. He began filling out the survey and was a bit short with the first two questions. He felt like he had more important things to do than fill out a preengagement survey for his soon-to-be coach. However, through the process, which seemed really reflective, he began to respond with a little more honesty to question number three. When he got to question number four, he wrote two words: *school culture*.

After completing the preengagement survey, he realized that Michelle Hebert would receive a notification because Survey Monkey alerts the person who created the survey after someone fills it out. He hurried and sent her a quick email response.

> Hi Dr. Hebert,
>
> I'm sorry for not returning your phone calls. I have been really swamped.
>
> I filled out the survey, and look forward to meeting you in a few days.
>
> Gavin

A few days later, Michelle went to Gavin's school. In the main office, she found Dr. Coppola waiting. Although Dr. Coppola did not want to spend a great deal of time there, she did want to be the one to introduce Michelle and Gavin. She spent about 15 minutes with them to help make them feel comfortable. They talked a bit about leadership. Dr. Coppola once again told Gavin that everyone can benefit from a good coach and that Michelle Hebert was at the top of the list when it came to coaches. She confided with Gavin that Michelle was her principal when she started out as an assistant principal and also acted as her coach. Gavin seemed to relax from the news.

However, after Dr. Coppola left the office, Gavin's body language changed. He sat back in his chair, crossed his arms, and fiddled with his smartphone. In his head, Gavin worried that his superintendent didn't think he was cut out for the job, even though Dr. Coppola assured him that was not the case.

Even though Michelle had coached Dr. Coppola, it was while they were principal and assistant principal, which is naturally how the relationship should be between a supervisor and new administrator. He then realized he certainly wasn't coaching his assistants.

Second, he was concerned about shifting the focus from being reactive to being proactive because his staff made it difficult for him to do so. One of his major goals was to place more focus on learning in the school and less on adults complaining about prep time, parent conflict, and other adult issues. However, all of those were part of the school culture long before he ever got there, which is why he answered number four with those two words.

Considering his insecurities, Gavin began worrying about his staff learning that he was working with a coach. Over and over he began wondering the following:

What would the staff think?

Should he tell them he has a coach?

If so, how should he tell them?

Coach's Corner

The Preengagement Survey

Regardless of whether you are a leadership coach or a principal trying to coach your assistant principals, send out a preengagement survey. Preengagement surveys allow time for the person on the receiving end to reflect and provide answers that could be beneficial to the leadership coach or the leader trying to coach.

LET GO OF COACHING MYTHS

Naylor Middle School has instructional coaches for teachers, which Gavin fully supports and even recommends on a regular basis, but he knew his status as a principal made the conversation different, right? He said those instructional coaches were for all teachers, but he knew it was really the struggling teachers that needed a coach. Would staff think he was ill-prepared for the job? Or would they respect him more because he was working with a coach? Over time, Gavin will hopefully learn that coaching is for everyone.

Michelle asked Gavin a lot of questions during their initial meeting. What Gavin didn't realize at the time, but certainly realized after he reflected, was that Michelle didn't do a lot of the talking. She let him do the talking and didn't even write one note. It was as though she really wanted to get to know him. As they engaged in dialogue, Michelle noticed that Gavin stayed in his same reclining position in his chair, with his arms folded, and he talked so fast that some of his sentences were incoherent.

What Gavin also didn't realize was that his answers and random outbursts provided a window into his mind frame as a leader. Michelle wanted to get to know him, check in with him over the next week or so, and then begin working on a goal for their leadership coaching experience. The three questions Michelle asked that stood out the most for Gavin during the conversation were as follows:

- *What do you want out of this coaching experience?*
- *What do you want out of your leadership?*
- *How do you evaluate your own impact at the same time you evaluate the impact of teachers?*

The first question was a bit hard to answer because he didn't fully know what he wanted out of coaching. It was the same question from the preengagement survey but he didn't have a better answer than he did a few days prior. He simply was not sure he needed a coach. Between the lawsuit from a parent, staff that were fighting with each other over things that didn't seem to be a big deal, and students saying they were being bullied, he wasn't even sure he had time to be coached.

Gavin's answer to the second question was that he hoped his leadership would lead to staff beginning to listen to him. The third question helped him realize that he didn't know the answer and wondered if Michelle did. Michelle told him not to answer any of the questions just yet and to take time to ponder them. She scheduled a meeting to return in two weeks, and her goal for the next meeting was to shadow Gavin for half a day.

After she left, Gavin thought about the meeting. Knowing that Michelle had coaching experience and was even his superintendent's supervisor made him feel a bit more at ease, but only time would tell how beneficial the coaching process would be. At some point Gavin would realize that Michelle had a great deal of valuable experience that he would be crazy not to learn from.

Coach's Corner

Sample Questions for Coaches to Ask Leaders

Whether you are a coach or a leader who is coaching assistant principals, the dialogue you inspire with those you coach is critically important. There are many great questions to ask, but the following are a few that you may be able to use to help you get to the heart of a quality coaching conversation.

- What do you want out of this experience?
- What would you see as your biggest success so far?
- What do you think is your biggest challenge?
- Would you be interested in working to improve the success or to overcome your challenge?
- If you could paint a picture of school leadership, what would it look like?
- If you could paint a picture of an ideal coaching relationship, what would that look like?
- When all is said and done, what are you hoping to gain from our coaching relationship?

Michelle Hebert—The Background Story

Michelle Hebert has been a leadership coach for about four years. After spending ten years as a teacher, seven years as a high school principal (where Dr. Coppola was her assistant), and three years as an assistant superintendent, she went into consulting to try something new and different.

She soon realized that the consultant world is fiercely competitive. While consultants talk a great deal about collaboration to school leaders and audiences, they are not necessarily very collaborative with each other. To avoid some of the cutthroat atmosphere, Michelle focused primarily on running workshops where she could get to know participants over a day or multiple days. She made it a point to send out a preengagement survey with three or four questions so she could gain an understanding of those participants she would be working with, and the participants enjoyed the fact that a consultant seemed to care about their voice, because Michelle would often discuss some of what they wrote in the anonymous surveys during the workshops. About two years into running workshops, she was asked to coach a few high school and middle school principals who were within their first years of leadership. Although she was a bit nervous about coaching, she realized it was really no different than how she approached working with her assistant principals when she was a high school principal. She loved the reciprocal learning that transpired over the time she worked with the principals. She learned as much from them as they did from her.

What surprised Michelle the most was when a superintendent reached out to her to ask if she would coach some principals within their district, and they would tell her that the principals were eager to be coached. Often, when she showed up for the first meeting with the principals, she quickly realized they had no desire to be coached. So when she met with Gavin the first time, she surmised that he was not open to coaching, although he never said anything to the contrary.

Michelle knew that her first steps were to build trust and foster a relationship. This was not rocket science. Her first conversations, and the words she chose during those conversations, all mattered. In her experience as a coach and a former school leader, she understood that there was more to coaching than just talking, but it involved body language and watching the person being coached in action as he or she interacted with staff and the school community. Being present and observant in the daily interactions was important, and that was what she would do with Gavin as well.

///

In the End

Michelle and Gavin had their first initial meeting. The preengagement survey was meant to garner some information from Gavin and to help put him at ease. When the superintendent joined the first meeting, she told Gavin that Michelle had coached her when she was the assistant principal and Michelle was her supervising principal. Although Gavin didn't necessarily show it, that information did make him feel a bit better.

The chapter also focuses on Gavin's self-esteem and insecurities. If you are leader and believe you have never felt insecure, you are not being honest with yourself. Everyone has insecurities. I have worked with leaders who allowed their insecurities to get the best of them, and they became hostile school leaders who expected compliance. I only wish they had worked with coaches so they could see the mistakes they were making. However, their mistakes were big learning opportunities for me as I went into leadership. I learned what not to do.

In the next chapter, you will learn the background story of another character and begin to see his role as a leader in a more complex and nuanced way. Let's face it—schools are complex organizations, and not every day is easy. These times of great conflict give us the opportunity to dig deep from our reserves and become better leaders.

DISCUSSION QUESTIONS

Coaches and Leaders:

- What do you see as Michelle's biggest challenge?
- How could you use a preengagement survey in your current role?

Leaders:

- Would you feel as insecure as Gavin if you were told to work with a coach?
- Gavin clearly doesn't feel comfortable in working with Michelle Hebert. How do you approach working through situations that make you uncomfortable?

Coaches:

- How do you introduce yourself to new principals who you will be coaching?
- How do you evaluate your own impact as a coach?
- Do you ever worry about your credibility when it comes to coaching?

TAKE ACTION

- Draft a preengagement survey that you can give to your next coachee.
- Draft a goal and develop a rubric to assess your progress toward that goal.

3

FOSTERING A SUPPORTIVE SCHOOL CLIMATE

When I speak about school climate, there are often people who say they feel like they do not have the time to put into it. They make it seem as though it is an add-on or something that they don't have any control over. However, I believe that school climate is the very plate that everything else sits on. Without a positive and supportive school climate, it is very difficult to foster academic and social–emotional growth.

There are many challenges in fostering a supportive school climate. One, if the principal doesn't get into classrooms and focus on learning, staff will most likely view that principal as someone who focuses solely on issues and discipline. After all, it's hard to receive feedback from a principal who doesn't actually step into the classroom.

We need leaders who will work collaboratively with staff and not expect staff to work collaboratively with each other as the principal sits in the office. We need leaders working side by side as much as they can. And yes, I understand that we have managerial things to take care of. When the boiler broke down in the building and it was 20 degrees outside, I couldn't ignore it so I could go into classrooms. However, we need a better balance between being an instructional leader and being a manager.

Another challenge is that we often talk about how students need to learn, but we don't often involve students in the process. As you read through this chapter, you will begin to see Gavin's growth as a leader and where he takes on challenges that will help in that growth. However, you will also be introduced to some ways to increase student voice in the school. If we aren't listening to students, are we really keeping their best interests in mind?

INTERACT WITH STUDENTS AND STAFF AT THE BEGINNING OF EACH DAY

Two weeks later Michelle Hebert returned for her appointment a bit early. She arrived before the school day officially began and was able to watch Gavin in action in the front entrance as she waited in the main office. In a few interactions he crossed his arms and seemed to jump into the conversation defensively, and in others he seemed to smile a bit more than usual and even laugh. It was clear that some staff made him feel comfortable while others put him on the defensive.

Michelle also noticed that Gavin interacted with students quite a bit. He high-fived a few, called others by name, and told a few he hoped he wouldn't see them for any negative reasons today. Gavin remembered one of the other pieces of student advice that his friend Sophie Murphy sent him through Voxer, which he hung on his office bulletin board and read before he walked out to meet the buses.

Gavin knew many of the students' names, and this was clearly a strength for him. Michelle realized that although Gavin may be spending too much time as manager, he was getting to know his students, and this made her feel a bit better as his coach. She overheard one of the students tell Gavin

A principal has to be someone that you trust. Someone who you can rely on to make your school great and someone that makes you laugh. They have to be nice and friendly. At assembly, recess, and lunch a good principal makes the children feel safe. All of the children listen to the principal and the principal doesn't have to yell for them to listen. They have to know how to lead the school and come into the classroom to see what the children are learning. Most importantly, and finally, they HAVE to know who you are.

Charlie 10 years old

Melbourne, Australia

that he was doing what she asked him to do when they met in the focus group, which is to smile more when students get off the bus. Michelle laughed a little when she heard the student mention focus groups, because listening to students is important, and putting into action the insight they provide is even more important.

EMPHASIZE THE POSITIVE

Once students settle in their classes, Michelle and Gavin sit down for their meeting. Michelle tells him how much she appreciates the effort he puts into knowing students. When they corresponded a few days prior through email, Gavin felt the need to tell her he was going to explore some student focus groups. He wanted her to know that he was not a failure in every part of his leadership, which Michelle already knew. He got the idea from Beth and wanted to have some evidence to use with teachers during a faculty meeting to show that not all students understand why they are learning what they are learning. Michelle admired Gavin's initiative in soliciting insights from students through focus groups, but she felt that his motives could use a bit of development.

"I liked the student focus group idea. What made you want to do that?" Michelle asks.

"I just wanted to get to know students, and I think it's important that they know their voices will be heard by me. I sent teachers an email after the last time we met and told them that I would be choosing students 8 and 9 from their class list for that period so I could ask them what they wanted out of their principal. My fear was that if I asked them to choose a student, they would choose the most articulate. So I randomly selected them by their number on the class list for that period," he explains.

Michelle smiles and agrees. "Did you get any feedback from teachers?" she asks. "Yeah, I felt like a few of them were pleasantly surprised and they kind of treated me differently, in a good way, from other times I had seen them," Gavin replies.

Michelle tells him that actions, like what he took with focus groups, are just as important as any words a principal may use.

Coach's Corner

Student Focus Groups

- Show students that you, as a leader, care about their voice.
- Select one or two students randomly from each class (depending on the size of your school) and ask them a few questions about what they want out of school, their teachers, and you as a leader.
- Gather the evidence and present it during a faculty meeting.

"I am planning to show the video compilation of the interviews at the next faculty meeting. I want them to understand that not all students know why they're learning what they're learning," he explains, almost with a twinge of arrogance.

"How do you think that will make staff feel? Do you think it will increase or decrease the trust issues you're all having?" Michelle asks.

Gavin understands her point and realizes that he was about to make a big mistake if he approached showing the video that way. "What do you suggest? Gavin asks.

Michelle explains that beginning with a positive is always important. Perhaps he could show the student interviews that were humorous at first and then the ones that are positive. She suggests he show a few of the negative interviews and then provide the percentages of students who could articulate learning and those who could not.

He realizes this is a much more collaborative approach than he was looking to take. Michelle asks Gavin for the purpose behind showing the video at the meeting.

He responds, "I want us to focus on engaging students, and when I walk into classrooms and look at our data, I can see we are not doing that to the extent we could."

"I think that is a good reason. I would just approach it from the idea that you are looking to use this as a baseline and then explore together ways to increase student engagement and voice," Michelle advises.

Gavin agrees that this is a better idea than his.

BE TRANSPARENT ABOUT THE COACHING

However, there is another big issue on Gavin's mind. He asks Michelle how he should approach the staff about his being coached. It seems to be an odd first question, which shows her that he has deep insecurities about working with her.

He confides in her that he is nervous about telling them he is working with a coach. "I mean, I'm fine with them knowing that I have a coach," Gavin begins stammering his words a bit, "but some of the things you and I will work on have to do with the culture of the building and not me as a leader," he adds.

"Whatever you decide is fine with me," Michelle says. "I'm here to work with you. I have to admit that I always find it best to be transparent. If leadership is about building trust with staff, then we should probably begin by being honest with them. After all, if they see you working with a coach, they may feel more comfortable when you suggest they work with a coach," Michelle adds. "Perhaps you begin with telling them about being coached at the faculty meeting and then go into the student learning video. That way they all know that you are looking to grow as a leader, and they may be more open to the student engagement conversation," Michelle explains.

Gavin understands her point and agrees with what she is saying; he just isn't fully on board with having a coach. Michelle knows it's time to push the envelope with Gavin a bit or they will not be able to move forward. She asks, "You seem nervous about telling staff. Do you mind if I ask why?"

"I'm just establishing trust with staff, and I don't want them to think I'm not competent," he replies, at the same time acknowledging that his video idea would have totally chipped away at the trust he says he so wants to build. He is quick to chime in and say, "Like I said before, some of these issues were here in the building long before I came here."

Michelle is about to ask a question and Gavin confides a little more. He tells her that Brad was passed over for the job, and Gavin feels he is undermining some of what Gavin is trying to do. This isn't the first time Michelle has run into an issue like this, but she wants to tread carefully because she knows Gavin isn't yet on board with being coached.

INVITE EVERYONE TO WORK TOWARD THE MISSION

"What role did Beth and Brad play in the student videos?" Michelle asks. Gavin looks down, pauses, and says, "Beth recorded the students but I didn't ask Brad to be a part of it because he didn't seem to want to."

"Did he say that he didn't want to be a part of it," Michelle asks. "No," Gavin answers.

Michelle explains that Brad will never step up to the plate and engage with Gavin if Gavin doesn't involve him in things. "Perhaps Brad is looking for an invitation," she says.

Gavin struggles with this idea a bit because he doesn't feel like he should have to coddle Brad. However, if he doesn't extend an olive branch, Brad may never truly engage.

"Ok. Let's address the first issue about the culture of the building. Sometimes being a leader is about dealing with the sins of the past, even if they are not your sins," Michelle says. "Keeping that in mind, isn't part of leadership about taking a difficult situation and improving it?" she asks. Her point is not one he can disagree with, and quite honestly, it causes him to sit back and think for a few seconds.

"Well, yes," Gavin replies. "But listen, Michelle. And I mean this respectfully. I have a lawsuit from a parent that stems from last year. The parent is saying the child didn't get the special education services they needed. I have pushback from a gender-neutral bathroom I created because I saw a need due to several students who identify as transgender that many teachers were not engaging, and I have a whole host of other issues between staff that all seem to be a direct result of bad leadership before me," Gavin confides. He doesn't mean to sound frustrated but he is indeed frustrated.

Coach's Corner

Improving the Culture of the School

Leaders fulfill their job of helping others come together and improving the culture of the school when they

- Foster relationships
- Empower staff
- Address the core culture issue
- Collectively define a focus with staff
- Stay focused
- Don't get caught up in the negativity and refocus on the positive

"Ok. Would you mind if we unpack that a bit?" Michelle asks. Gavin nods in agreement.

"The lawsuit. Are you getting help from the director of special education?" Michelle asks.

"Yes, it's just I feel badly that this happened. I've met the parents and they're untrusting of me because I'm the principal, but I'm trying to get to know them," Gavin explains.

"Well, what are some other things you can do where that is concerned?" Michelle asks.

"I talked with staff about making sure they read the IEP because it's a legal document. Not something I thought I would have to do. I am also making sure I meet with the special education team on a weekly basis," Gavin explains.

"Gavin, that's a good place to start. It sounds like the parents are receptive to meeting with you, and the director of special education is talking through the lawsuit."

"What about the transgender issue?" Michelle asks.

"That's a nonnegotiable for me. It's a law in the state that we have to protect all students. But I want to do more than protect. I want to know that we are including them and making all students feel welcome. I mean, do you know that LGBT students are at high risk of dropping out of school?" Gavin asks with a bit of fire in his face.

Michelle nods her head in agreement, and Gavin can tell that she is on his side on this one. Michelle is actually impressed because Gavin is showing some serious leadership and standing up first for students, even when some staff and parents don't agree.

As for Brad, what are your thoughts on why he is acting the way he is?" Michelle asks. "Well, he got passed over for the lead job in a school he taught in for six years and has been an assistant principal for five," Gavin answers. "I just always felt that leadership is about showing who you are when you don't get the job as much as when you do get the job," Gavin says.

Michelle thinks that is a profound statement and can see why Dr. Coppola has high hopes for Gavin.

Brad's Story

Brad Washington was a victim of his own circumstances. As a new assistant principal, he was eager to collaborate with staff and make an impact on students. Each day that he entered the building was a new opportunity to grow, but his enthusiasm was soon dampened by Principal Alan Johnson. Alan, the principal who ran the building before Gavin, was not collaborative at all. When Brad arrived at his desk each morning he found a pile of discipline referrals. Principal Johnson insisted on looking them over before giving them to Brad. As much as Brad wanted to get into the classrooms to guide and assist teachers, he was relegated to "doing discipline." Over time, this extinguished any fire within him.

After his first year, Brad began looking for jobs as a principal within his district and other districts as well. Due to lower enrollment and budget cuts, few jobs were opening, and the ones that did open offered a trial by fire experience that he was not willing to experience. As the years went on, he found himself less and less eager to try to make a difference.

It is not that Alan's leadership, or lack thereof, was a surprise to Brad, because he had worked there as a teacher before he became the assistant; but he thought that being in leadership was a secret society and Alan would be different behind closed doors. He wasn't. Alan was temperamental on some days and evasive on others. So when Alan announced he was retiring, Brad was overjoyed with the prospect of taking over Naylor Middle School, only to be disappointed again, because Alan said he would put in a good word for Brad but never did.

Brad interviewed for the position but realized he couldn't answer some of the questions search committee members asked, so he walked out of the interview defeated and embarrassed. And then the committee announced that it was hiring an outsider named Gavin Young. Brad told himself he would keep looking for new positions in other districts.

Dive Into the Difficult Conversations

At the end of the school day, Brad sees a woman leave Gavin's office. He had seen her before at Shaw Elementary School. The woman was walking around with the principal of Shaw, and Brad thought he overheard someone mention that she was a leadership coach. There were no secrets among teachers in a school, especially when it involved the school principal. Brad was a bit taken aback to see her at Naylor Middle with Gavin.

A few minutes after she leaves, Gavin enters Brad's office. Beth had already left for an appointment, and the two begin talking about the trials and tribulations of the day. Gavin can sense that Brad is in a mood to talk, so he tells him that he is being coached by Michelle Hebert. Brad seems surprised that Gavin would have to work with a coach, considering he got the job over Brad, and Gavin steps out of his comfort zone to delve into a much-needed conversation with Brad.

"I know that you are probably wondering why I need a coach if I got the job," Gavin says, as Brad sits, not moving or saying anything. "The truth is I'm not really crazy about it yet either, but I have some things I need to work on and I think Michelle can help," Gavin continues.

Brad simply says, "That's good," and shakes his head.

Gavin doesn't stop there. "I know you have been upset that you didn't get the job," he says.

"Well, I was here for six years as a teacher and five as an assistant. Wouldn't you take that a bit as a slap in the face?" Brad asks, sitting up a bit straighter.

"Yes, I would," Gavin agrees, "but I may also take it as a learning experience." Brad doesn't say anything. "Sometimes we learn a lot about ourselves when we don't get what we want, and we can move forward or retreat. I'd really like to work with you on moving forward. I really feel like we can do some great things as a team, if you will work with me," Gavin explains.

"It's a lot to think about," Brad says.

"I know, but it's also how we can move the school forward. This sort of wedge we have isn't going to help either of us," Gavin says. Brad sits back and stays silent. "Bottom line for me is that I need you fully in," and with a sensitive look, Gavin gets up and walks to his office.

A few minutes later Brad walks into the office to say goodnight and tells Gavin not to stay too late. Gavin takes that as a sign that they are moving in the right direction. He then picks up the phone and calls Beth to explain that he is working with a coach. Brad walks out of the building feeling as though he needs to keep his options open. Time will tell whether Gavin would suffer the same fate of lackluster leadership that his predecessor exhibited.

///

Embrace Vulnerability

"Well, I think leadership is also about stepping out of your comfort zone and putting yourself in a vulnerable position so others can follow suit, even if there are others who may try to use it against you," Michelle says.

"I will figure out a way to include Brad in all of this," Gavin says.

Michelle does not realize yet that Gavin really does not want to work with her. However, Gavin is beginning to like the challenge that Michelle offered. He agrees with what she said, but it still scares him a bit to make himself vulnerable in front of others. He sits back and waits for her to continue the dialogue. He really doesn't have much to offer, because he isn't sure why he is in this predicament.

"Why did you want to work with a coach if you're concerned about what staff would think?" Michelle asks. It is a poignant question, and Gavin lacks a poker face, so he can't soften his answer.

"I didn't want to work with you … I mean a coach," Gavin answers. "Dr. Coppola suggested it to me, and I couldn't say no because she's my boss." Gavin adds.

"Fair enough," Michelle replies. "Do you find value in coaching?" she asks.

"Well, yes. Of course. I was a competitive runner in high school and college, and my coaches had a huge impact on me as an athlete and as a person," Gavin says.

"So why is this different? If we can work together, might our relationship help you grow as a leader?" Michelle asks. "Listen, Gavin, I'm not here to tell you what to do. Just like with instructional coaching, I'm here to watch what you do and help you with a goal you choose, and I would like to learn from you as well," she says.

There is really no going back now for Gavin. Michelle raises a good point about leadership, and he realizes he was spending a little too much time blaming his predecessor. Although he thought there were issues of culture that happened before he got there, he knew that he was hired to be an instructional leader, which was going to take collaboration and trust. He was just worried that Michelle was going to expect compliance and that she was going to be a confidant of Dr. Coppola. It's not that he didn't trust Dr. Coppola, but if the coaching relationship was going to work, he didn't want it to be all focused on compliance to district mandates and initiatives, because some of that was sucking the fun out of his job already. He had heard horror stories from friends on the Voxer group that leadership coaches are used as compliance officers.

BELIEVE IN YOUR OWN CAPABILITY

"Have you heard of self-efficacy?" Michelle asks.

"Of course," Gavin replies politely.

"What can you tell me about it?" Michelle asks, calling his bluff a bit.

Gavin realizes at that moment that he knows the words but not necessarily the definition. "It's a belief we have in ourselves," he replies quickly, as if the answer just popped into his head. He and Michelle laugh a little bit by the way he answers.

"Absolutely," Michelle says. "It's the confidence to take action (Bandura, 1997), and no one can feel efficacious in every part of their job (Tschannen-Moran & Gareis, 2004)," she explains.

"None of us have confidence in every aspect of the job, and efficacy is really difficult to raise. In fact, I saw Tom Guskey speak one time, and he said that there are three pieces to raising self-efficacy. Number 1 is that we have to have a protocol in place. Coaching, whether it's the coaching we are doing or instructional coaching your teachers are experiencing, would be considered a protocol in place," Michelle begins.

As Michelle talks, Gavin begins taking notes.

She continues by saying, "the second important element to raising efficacy is that the person trying to raise their efficacy needs to have evidence they trust. So, after we define the goal we need to talk about evidence that you trust or we will not be able to move forward as strongly as we could," she says.

Gavin continues taking notes.

"What's the third component," Gavin asks.

Michelle can see that Gavin is beginning to get drawn in. She is building credibility and giving him something to think about that he could actually put into action fairly immediately. Michelle's conversation is a good balance between the pulling along of Gavin to build trust and the pushing forward to get him to stop the blame game with his predecessor. Michelle knows this is not the end of Gavin's resistance, but it is a good win for leadership coaching.

"Well, the third component is seeing an improvement within weeks and not months. We need a little more instant gratification these days," Michelle says with a smile. Gavin sits back in his chair, definitely agreeing with that thought. He is feeling a little less patient these days.

"Seriously, we can't wait months and months to see improvement. We need to see the fruits of our efforts a little quicker. So we need to make sure we gain evidence you trust and you see benefits sooner than later. Does that make sense?" Michelle asks.

Gavin agrees with everything Michelle is saying. He has to admit that he is feeling a bit better about coaching.

Coach's Corner

Self-Efficacy Review

We raise our self-efficacy when we

- Have a protocol in place
- Collect evidence we trust (valid and reliable evidence)
- See improvement within weeks and not months (T. Guskey, personal communication, May 8, 2017)

IMPROVE THE CLIMATE FIRST, THEN THE CULTURE

"We can work on having an effect on the culture, after we begin doing things that affect the climate," Michelle says.

"How do we do that?" Gavin asks.

"We begin working on consistently greeting teachers and students in the morning. I was really impressed by how many of the students' names you know," Michelle says.

Harper (2012) explained the use of the word *minoritized* instead of *minority:*

Persons are not born into a minority status nor are they minoritized in every social context (e.g., their families, racially homogeneous friendship groups, or places of worship). Instead, they are rendered minorities in particular situations and institutional environments that sustain an overrepresentation of Whiteness. (p. 9)

Gavin replies that he had been studying the yearbook from the year before to help him remember more names.

Michelle is even more impressed after hearing that. "That's really incredible, Gavin."

Regarding climate, Michelle continues, "In addition to studying yearbooks it is important to hang images in the hallway that reflect the students in the school. Students need an emotional connection to the school, but I don't see a lot of images that would engage them. Those images should include minoritized populations as well."

Gavin's facial expression shows that he clearly agrees with Michelle. They talk for a bit about how to foster a more inclusive school climate that will, in time, have a more positive effect on school culture.

Coach's Corner

Fostering an Inclusive School Climate

- We love images. It's why Facebook, Instagram, and other types of social media are so popular. We need to see images that make us comfortable. All students need to see images that reflect their lives. Make sure those images are student made and visible in the hallways. Make sure that the books and curriculum reflect the experiences of the students in the school.
- Principals greet students into the school. Teachers greet students into classes.
- Use common language that focuses on learning (i.e., self-regulation, resilience).
- Avoid educational acronyms when talking with parents. This creates a disconnection with parents.

Michelle tells Gavin the focus for the half day is to get a feel for his leadership style and see how he interacts with staff, students, and parents. She also hopes to have a conversation regarding setting a goal. Michelle explains that coaching can be very one-sided if it's done in isolation, where the coach only meets with the principal in the office and doesn't spend quality time seeing the principal in action with stakeholders. As the students change classes, Michelle once again notices that Gavin says good morning and knows many of their names, which is important because it helps students feel engaged in their school community when the principal knows their names.

As the morning progresses, Michelle and Gavin walk around the hallways engaging with students, and they even go into a few different homerooms before the morning announcements. She notices that Brad and Beth are not in the hallways they enter and asks Gavin if he knows where they are this time of day. Gavin explains that Brad is in his office, and Beth is in classrooms doing walk-throughs. Michelle thinks she might revisit this during a later conversation. She

Coach's Corner

Coaching and School Climate

When shadowing a school leader, coaches should keep a look out for indications of the state of the school climate.

- How many names does the leader know?
- What images are displayed around the campus?
  - Are the images representative of the student population (i.e., race, gender, sexual orientation)?
  - Are they professionally created or created by students?
- How friendly and engaging is the school secretary?
- Do the students look excited to be there?
- Are learning intentions and success criteria visibly displayed?
- How many classrooms does the leader go into? Does it seem as though the leader greets students and visits classes consistently or only when the coach is present?
- What are the conversations between the adults about? For example, when Gavin gets stopped by a teacher, is it to talk about learning or behavior?

also notices that some of the teachers are giving her the once-over because they do not know who she is, and Gavin hasn't made any introductions.

Gavin starts to feel a little less anxious each time Michelle speaks. She is not new to coaching and realizes she needs to feed Gavin a lot of positive feedback so that he will engage with her a little more and trust the coaching process. She also understands that Gavin is at a very critical point in the trust-building process with her, and she wants to make sure she spends more time on positives than negatives.

Through the conversation, Michelle finds out that Beth is responsible for sixth grade, and Brad is responsible for seventh grade. Although Gavin has responsibility over the whole school, eighth grade is the grade level where he spends the most time. Eventually, Gavin and Michelle make their way back to his office.

As they sit down for one last conversation before Michelle leaves, she looks at him and asks, "Where do you want to start?" This is something he has pondered in the last week but couldn't get past his insecurities about coaching. Michelle brings up the topic of thinking about the end in mind. She asks the following ("Coach's Corner") questions.

Coach's Corner

Where Do You Want to Start?

- In what area of your leadership do you want to be more collaborative? (The goal of **collaborative coaching** is for leaders to be more collaborative with stakeholders, which will ultimately have a positive effect on student learning.)
- In what areas do you need to be more collaborative?
- What evidence will you collect to help you get a better sense of your level of collaborative leadership?
- Is the collaboration you engage in authentic, or is it really just compliant engagement where you expect teachers to follow your lead?

Michelle is working with two other administrators in a neighboring district. She tells Gavin she would like him to think about the questions and she will be back in a week. She says she feels that one week is a sufficient amount of time for him to ponder the questions and come up with a few goals that they can then talk through in their meeting. She also reminds him that she is only a phone call or email away.

Before she leaves, however, she wants to address one more issue. "Listen, Gavin," she begins. He looks up and waits to hear what she has to say. "I think you may need to look at Brad through a different lens."

"What do you mean?" Gavin asks.

"You know he got passed over for the job, and that is definitely on your mind because you said it several times," she continues ever so politely. "The reality is that Brad may be acting the way he has always been allowed to act as a teacher and assistant principal. Perhaps you're the one who can show him another way to lead," and that is where she stops.

Michelle's insight definitely gives Gavin something to think about. Although he isn't sure that Brad is open to it, Gavin also knows that he is stuck with him for at least a year, and they need to make it work.

WHERE SHOULD GAVIN START?

Gavin understands that anywhere he starts will need to begin with trust building, because teachers in the building are not used to authentic collaboration. Truthfully, Gavin isn't either and there will be more mistakes to come that will help him figure out just how important trust and the sins of the past are when leading a building.

Gavin does an excellent job of building trust with students, but the adults are proving to be a little more difficult. What he is learning is that he needs to do the same thing with teachers that he does with students. Greeting people at the

Coach's Corner

Ways to Strengthen a Collaborative Culture

- **Faculty meetings**—Instead of a checklist of items, do you want your faculty meetings to be more like professional development sessions?
- **Teacher observations**—Instead of a one and done, would you like to set goals and provide effective feedback to teachers, as opposed to visiting their classroom for 45 minutes without any mutual understanding of what you may be looking for in the teaching and learning that takes place?
- **PLCs**—Are the PLCs in your school spaces where teachers can challenge each other's thinking and go from surface-level to deep-level learning in one area that focuses on a problem of practice?
- **Student relationships**—Do you want to strengthen your relationships with students so they do not just look at you as the disciplinarian but as someone who will help them?
- **Family engagement**—Many times schools tell families what they want from them (i.e., attend the open house, chorus concerts, parent–teacher conferences, etc.). Family engagement should be about the dialogue that takes place between families and schools to strengthen the relationship.
- **The leadership team**—There are times, such as at the beginning of this book, where principals work in isolation from their assistants. Coaching could help leaders understand how important it is to work as a team.

door, knowing their names, and making them feel welcome are all places to begin. Focusing on a goal that will cause an impact on student learning will get easier after the relationships are established.

As he reflects on where to go next, he searches online and finds a blog that focuses on providing student perspectives on what principals should do. He reads a post by two middle school students, which helps him see that he is moving in the right direction.

Make People Feel Comfortable

Lila and Zoe, sixth-grade students

Burbank, CA

We've really both only had two principals before; at least that we remember. One of which (our elementary school principal) started her term the year we began kindergarten, so it was like we were going through the new experience of elementary together with her. She was one of the most kind-hearted and brilliant people we had ever met. She managed to be powerful, yet also welcoming. Not only was she capable of greeting everyone by name, but could also simultaneously plan the smartest fundraisers.

Once every year at our elementary school, there is a fundraiser called the Fall Festival. During the Fall Festival, you can enter a raffle to win a prize, play fun games, hang out with friends, and eat from food trucks. One year there was a chance to win the pleasure of eating lunch with your principal, which we ended up winning.

Being shy, young kids, we will admit that we entered her room a bit cautiously. We didn't want to make a wrong move or say the wrong thing, after all she was the principal! After sitting down and making conversation, we grew to realize we had nothing to fear. She told us stories, she got us lunch, she made us laugh, and best of all, she made us feel comfortable around her, which is all we could really ask for in a principal. We want someone that we can easily talk to, but someone who also manages to be authoritative. To this day, we still keep in touch with her, regardless of the fact that we are now in middle school. She even leads our book club. No matter how scared we were going into elementary school, she managed to make it some of the best years of our lives.

Studies show that the first day of middle school is the hardest school day of our entire life—that includes college. As the two of us walked through the gates of our new middle school, this fact soon seemed to become true, until our new principal greeted us into the school. She was so sweet and seemed to understand exactly what was going through our heads at that moment.

We are only halfway through our first year of middle school, and already feel extremely comfortable with our new school, thanks to our principal. This is due to the fact that she tries to get to know us, and really understands what it's like to be new.

We believe that principals should be kind, understanding, and powerful. We want someone who tries to relate to us, yet also shows discipline when needed. Principals are key to a well-functioning school. It is important for them to be the best they can be!

In the End

- If you, as a leader, want your teachers to benefit from coaching relationships, it is important that you establish a climate of self-improvement and growth where you set the example by being transparent about your own needs for leadership PLCs and a leadership coach.
- Establish a culture of improvement by being proactive rather than reactive.
- As a leadership coach, be sure you take the time to get to know your coachee before jumping ahead to establishing a goal.
- Ask good questions to get at the heart of the issues rather than addressing surface problems.
- To establish a collaborative culture, try to look at resistant staff members through a new lens. Begin to rethink your interactions with them. Trust them enough to hold them to a higher standard.

As we move on through the story of Gavin and Michelle, you will see the ebb and flow of their relationship, as well as the introduction of real issues and new faces. As an experienced coach, it is vitally important that Michelle looks at each time they have together in their defined relationship as an opportunity to go deeper and help Gavin build capacity. Coaching is about empowering leaders to the point that they would rather build synergy and make improvements with their staff than be meeting with a coach.

Where Gavin is concerned, you will begin to see him take on the leadership role with much more confidence, and some of that will lead into his coaching of Beth and Brad. We need strong and sensitive leadership these days, and Gavin is the one to help us get there.

DISCUSSION QUESTIONS

Coaches and Leaders:

- Have you ever had insecurities like Gavin? If yes, how did you overcome them?
- Do you believe that Michelle offered good insights about Brad? Explain your answer.
- What did you learn from the student voices in this chapter? What are your thoughts on their insights?

Leaders:

- Would you work with a leadership coach? Why or why not?
- How would you approach your staff about working with a coach?
- What could a coach help you learn that you may be unable to learn on your own or with staff?
- How might you use some of Michelle's approaches with your assistant principals?
- Would you have had a similar conversation that Gavin did with Brad if you were in his position?
- Have you been passed over for a job you firmly believed you should have been given? How did you handle the disappointment?

Coaches:

- What do you bring to the coaching relationship? What makes you special?
- What do you want to learn in the coaching process?

TAKE ACTION

- Send out a survey to your students and staff asking how they would characterize the school climate. Use some of the questions from "Coach's Corner: Coaching and School Climate" (p. 48).
- In collaboration with your staff, create a goal addressing one way to improve school climate. Together make a plan to carry out that goal. The plan should include a way to assess progress and benchmarks toward the goal.
- Each week, get to know two students you don't already know.

GAVIN BECOMES MORE **OPEN** TO COACHING

S ome might believe that the coaching process involves an immediate setting of a goal that focuses on student learning, even for those of us coaching at the leadership level. However, what I have learned is that there are times when the most important goal is relationship building. This is not rocket science, nor is it information you haven't heard before. As coaches and leaders, feel free to avoid the pressure to jump into a student learning goal if it is not actually the best goal at the present time.

In the unfolding story between Gavin and Michelle, we have learned that Gavin was not all that enthusiastic about being coached. It took weeks for Michelle to get to know Gavin and gain his trust. Having coached before, Michelle knew that there is a fine balance between pushing for an impactful goal and building a relationship with the person being coached. The onus was on her to make sure she offered Gavin something valuable that he could learn from during each coaching session.

As a leadership coach, it's important for me to listen to the leaders I coach and offer them simple practical steps that they can use after we finish our conversation. For example, there are leaders who talk about their faculty meetings and how they give information to their staff and are then met with silence. They refer to it as crickets. I suggest they send the information ahead of time so staff can seek out some surface-level knowledge prior to the meeting. When sending information out, leaders might consider adding three questions for the staff to think about and suggest that staff come to the meeting with two questions of their own. This advice is an example of an immediate strategy that leaders can act on as soon as the coaching session is over. In addition to a strategy, I also highlight the common themes in the conversation as a way of summarizing and aiding us both in thinking about a larger goal we can design together.

WHAT IT MEANS TO BE MORE OPEN TO COACHING

Over the first month of their relationship, Gavin became more accustomed to the idea of coaching. Michelle was easy to talk with and offered great insights. But he still worried about what she would be telling Dr. Coppola. After all, it was Dr. Coppola who wanted him to be coached. Would their relationship truly be confidential?

Although Gavin was insecure about letting his staff know about the coaching he was receiving, as he became more positive about the coaching experience, he decided to take the plunge and tell them. Many of them were supportive, while a few looked at each other and made some comments that seemed negative. Not all teachers like their administrators. Some feel that administrators left the classroom to "go to the dark side." Therefore, there are bound to be some staff members who would characterize Gavin's need for a coach as a weakness rather than a strength.

Later on, he heard Brad saying to one staff member that the coaching experience was a good thing because he was learning through the experience as well. Gavin felt reassured hearing that sentiment from Brad. Actually, Brad began to see the negative comments on the part of some staff as an unfortunate circumstance rather than an opportunity to get Gavin out so he could take the position. He found himself supporting Gavin and coming to his defense. Brad was further bolstered by the observation that Gavin seemed to be open to some of Brad's feedback as well.

From the first encounter with Michelle, it took Gavin a few weeks to come up with a more established goal, but in the meantime he and Michelle had actually worked on quite a bit already. Gavin began to find that his effort to build relationships and foster a team among his assistant principals all fit into the greater goal that he was about to formally establish with Michelle. Without trust and relationship building, very few initiatives or goals would ever be successful.

Gavin realized he had low expectations of Brad because he knew Brad had been passed over for the job and was upset about it. But after his conversation with Michelle about Brad, Gavin consciously took a different path and began giving Brad more responsibility. His philosophy was that if Brad wanted his own principalship, it was time to start helping him work toward that goal.

Gavin became less anxious in areas of leadership and began talking to staff individually about hanging pictures in the hallways to create a warmer environment, one where all students feel included. He suggested images that reflect the school's diverse student population. He remained very engaged with students and started to seek out some of his harder-to-reach students, like those suffering from trauma and the minoritized populations.

Before Michelle and Gavin talked about the goal Gavin was to focus on, she said they first needed to set some ground rules. Setting a goal and working toward it is merely one step in the coaching process. Michelle knew they needed to set up some nonnegotiable items. After all, an administrator's life is never the same from day to day. Between student issues, teacher demands, and the daily running of a school, Michelle understood that the best intentions can get lost if some parameters aren't set.

As much as they connected in person, Michelle knew that during the time they were not together, Gavin was at risk of taking steps back into the land of insecurity. It's easy to revert to old habits, even if those habits were learned due to the previous administrator's bad decisions. Ground rules would help Gavin feel more secure in moving forward with a coach.

Coach's Corner

Set Ground Rules

- As a coach, or a leader coaching assistant principals, what are your nonnegotiable items?
  - What goals should leaders work on?
  - How should they collect evidence to understand their impact?
  - Are there specific priorities leaders should work on?
- What ground rules are important for you during a coaching conversation (i.e., turn off cell phone, define a set of questions ahead of time, etc.)?
- What is the ideal length of a coaching conversation? Does it matter?

Michelle begins talking to Gavin about being open to coaching. At this point, Gavin takes a step back, because he thought he was engaged, so he isn't sure what it is about his responses or body language that is making Michelle feel he isn't open to coaching. Michelle can tell what Gavin is thinking by the way he shifts in his seat when she mentions it.

"No, it's not what you're thinking," Michelle says. "I just mean *open* as an acronym. We need to set up some parameters." Michelle explains what the acronym means (see Figure 4.1):

Opportunity—There needs to be an authentic **opportunity** to coach. This means that when they set up a meeting,

Figure 4.1   OPEN to Coaching

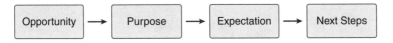

they are both completely present during their time together. There should be no phones or time spent on the computer. If this means that Michelle needs to meet with Gavin after school when things calm down a bit, she will do that. She also understands that emergencies happen in a school and that Gavin's first responsibility is to make sure kids are safe.

Michelle wants to establish a time with Gavin where they can meet without interruption. Gavin sees this as a positive because he wants to be fully present, and he realizes this is a good time to provide Beth and Brad with the opportunity to take more responsibility with staff.

Gavin assures Michelle that he will commit to the time they schedule as long as there isn't a catastrophe happening in the school. He also lets her know that, if done correctly, this is going to be a true partnership.

Purpose—There needs to be **purpose** behind coaching. There are so many great ideas in education that begin with good intentions and then through miscommunication, competing priorities, and a lack of authentic purpose, those ideas are swept to the side, or worse, become a checklist of items that participants check off and say have been completed.

Purpose is necessary when it comes to coaching, which is why it's necessary for the leader to choose the best goal for them and their school community. Where will the coaching relationship focus so that student learning and teaching strategies become a priority? Is it the faculty meeting, classroom observations, or those walk-throughs that can be beneficial but have already been done? We shouldn't bother getting into the coaching relationship if the goal lacks purpose.

Coach's Corner

Walk-Throughs

Walk-throughs are supposed to bring about a common language and understanding of what teachers and leaders want when it comes to student learning. Students can also be involved in the walk-through process. Unfortunately, walk-throughs often become something leaders do *to* teachers as opposed to *with* them.

Many leaders walk in to classrooms checking through a list of desired activities or characteristics that may or may not have been shared with the teacher prior to the classroom observation. If the leader does not share the list with the teacher before and after the observation, it is unlikely that the walk-through will provide the teacher with useful feedback regarding what he or she is doing well and also what can be improved. Furthermore, walk-throughs seldom focus on students and student learning; instead, they focus on what adults are doing or not doing.

Setting Up a Walk-Through:

For walk-throughs to be purposeful, there are some necessary elements that need to be included in the process. Those elements are:

Provide Feedback: Leaders need to be able to provide feedback during the walk-through. If they don't, teachers will continue to believe that walk-throughs are done *to* them instead of *with* them. In order for feedback to stick, it needs to be wrapped around a goal that teachers care about and a conversation involving how the goal will look if it is met with success. Overall, this means that the goal of the lesson and the successful completion of the goal need to be discussed before the walk-through occurs.

If leaders are doing a building walk-through and they want all teachers to be achieving the same goal, that goal and the conditions of success need to be established at a faculty meeting. If this does not happen before the walk-through, the teachers are being set up for failure.

Use a Walk-Through Tool: In Iowa, where collaborative leadership work has been adopted at the state level, one assistant principal discussed a tool he uses for his walk-throughs. It's called Penultimate. Penultimate is a digital handwriting app that can be downloaded on a tablet. A leader can set up folders for each teacher and then take notes and upload pictures from the classroom. The assistant principal from Iowa set up folders for each teacher, which housed each teacher's goal. As he went from room to room for walk-throughs, he took pictures and wrote notes that he uploaded to each teacher's folder and then shared the folders with the teachers. His goal was to keep the feedback flowing around each goal.

Ditch the Checklist: We should ditch the checklists associated with walk-throughs. They set up a dynamic where leaders talk down to teachers, and they are rarely used to develop dialogue around student learning between the adults associated with those walk-throughs.

Improve the Process: The only way to improve the walk-through process is to continue an ongoing dialogue about the process at staff meetings. Walk-throughs should focus on the impact teachers are having on student learning, which should include constant reflection, collecting of evidence, and a continuation of the formal teacher observation process. Staff meetings, walk-throughs, and teacher observation should all be aligned.

To continue the dialogue around being OPEN, Michelle explains the last two steps to Gavin.

Expectation—The **expectation** needs to be that the coaching cycle will change beliefs and behavior. It's not enough to just go through the coaching cycle to say we did it. It's important that when the coaching cycle is complete, the leader is on a new path toward being a more collaborative leader. Both the coach and the leader need to understand that quality coaching provides the opportunity to build collective efficacy. One of the biggest contributors to collective efficacy is vicarious experiences, which means we all have the opportunity to learn from each other when the partnership is right. However, educational researcher John Hattie says in his keynote speeches that part of that learning requires that collective efficacy be fed with evidence of impact. Coach and leader must be collecting evidence through this coaching cycle. In the beginning of any coaching relationship, the leader and coach need to set expectations, and the leader should always work hard to exceed those expectations.

Next—What will be the **next** step after the coaching is complete? If we are all truly lifelong learners, then we need to start thinking of next steps at the end of the coaching cycle. The next steps may involve the following:

- Choosing a new goal
- Taking the completed goal and extending it to make it stronger and more impactful
- Taking the completed goal and using it in another subject area or with another grade level
- Always thinking of next steps when we achieve a goal after going through a coaching cycle

WHOSE AGENDA IS THIS?

When it comes to goal setting, Michelle works hard to ensure that she does not impose her own agenda on the leaders and that they choose their own goals. Principals who work in a coaching role with their assistant principals should follow the same rule. This is not always easy for a coach or principal taking the coaching role, because typically both parties walk

---

Coach's Corner

Understand Your Coachee's Needs

When establishing goals, the following steps will help the coach understand the needs of the leader he or she is working with:

- The coach asks questions that will get to the heart of the leader's needs to determine the best goal for that leader.
- The coach objectively approaches the relationship so as to focus on the leader's agenda.
- The coach approaches the relationship with the understanding that coaching should offer reciprocal learning on the part of the coach and the individual being coached (Knight, 2007).
- The coach does not manipulate the relationship to get what he or she wants.

into a coaching relationship with a great deal of experience from the road and they know some of the areas all leaders need to work on. Although those conversations can still come up between a coach and a leader, Michelle understands that it's important for coaches to suspend their own thinking and replace it with more of an open mind to help the leader find his or her best goal.

A few days prior to meeting with Michelle, Gavin sits down and reviews the following collaborative leadership growth cycle (see Figure 4.2). He needs the visual to map out his thinking. Gavin finds himself floating between a few goals and wants to make sure he chooses the one that will be most impressive to Michelle. He wants to "get the right answer." Gavin will eventually realize this is not what Michelle is looking for, and it certainly isn't what coaching is all about.

When using the collaborative leadership growth cycle, there is a process that the leader and the coach need to follow to ensure growth takes place:

Goal Setting—The leader needs to focus on one specific situation in his or her leadership. Through the goal-setting

Figure 4.2   Collaborative Leadership Cycle

process, the coach can shadow the leader to provide the necessary feedback to ensure the leader is choosing the right goal. Ultimately, this goal should revolve around learning and focus on increasing the self-efficacy of staff, building collective efficacy among staff, and increasing the leader's ability to work collaboratively with others.

If leaders want teacher observations to be more effective, they need to change the way they approach the process. The coach can work through what an effective teacher observation should look like. The following are important elements of an effective teacher observation:

- *Setting Goals*—The teacher chooses a goal for the observation (i.e., teaching strategy, student–teacher relationships, etc.). In this conversation, the teacher and leader establish how it will be successful, also known as success criteria. Establishing success criteria is necessary because the feedback the leader will give is centered around it.
- *Sharing Resources*—The leader finds resources to help the teacher meet his or her goal at the same time the leader finds resources that will help both of them be successful. Perhaps it's the use of articles and blogs or a Teaching Channel video that shows what the successful delivery will look like. When a leader helps teachers find resources they care about, the process helps the leader as much as the teachers.
- *Observing*—The leader goes in with the established goal and success criteria and observes the teacher. However, most of the leader's time is spent talking with students, because we believe that the students should be the focus of our observation. If students know what they are learning and why they are learning it, then it is most likely an effective lesson.
- *Providing Feedback*—The leader provides feedback regarding the goal and success criteria in a postobservation setting. If the teacher has something to improve on where the goal is concerned, the leader provides insight into what that might be. However, the

teacher is equally responsible for understanding what that improvement might look like as well.

- *Observing Again*—If the teacher needs to work on one element to show improvement, the leader goes back into the classroom to observe. This additional observation might not be a part of the established observation process as much as it is a part of the walk-through process the leader might engage in.

Current Reality—The next step for the leader and coach is to understand their current reality in that specific situation. This process of understanding the current reality is where the coach provides feedback to the leader on which leadership style he or she might be using. There are four leadership styles:

- *Bystanders*—These leaders don't define any positive goals, and they don't inspire stakeholders to collaborate. They have low growth performance and low partnership qualities. Teachers work in silos and the principal remains in his or her office with few attempts at visibility.
- *Regulators*—These leaders define the goal for the teacher and the school. Although they have high performance, they control the whole environment. These leaders know what idea they want to walk out of a meeting with well before they ever walk into the meeting. Unfortunately, they do not inspire true partnerships around the school as much as they promote compliance, which ultimately creates a hostile school climate where teachers wait to be told what to do.
- *Negotiators*—Negotiators seem as though they are inspiring collaboration but what they do is define the goal behind closed doors and then slowly make their way around the school or district and get people on board with their ideas. They create coalitions. This works just as long as stakeholders believe in the goal, rather than feel they have to achieve it because it's coming from the top.
- *Collaborators*—These leaders find the perfect balance between inspiring stakeholders to collaborate and

co-constructing building and classroom-level goals. They believe in a high level of transparency and honesty and have a high level of performance because stakeholders feel as though they have a voice in the process.

Evidence Gathering—After leaders understand their current reality, they will do some evidence gathering to help them reflect on past practice and understand how to move forward. Leaders can collect evidence through surveys or interviews with a well-rounded group that will provide the leader with honest answers or artifacts of learning. The following questions might be asked during this process to help the leader:

- What are the learning needs of our school?
- What are my individual learning needs?
- What are the required changes?
- How do we implement the improvement?

Action Step—After leaders go through the evidence-gathering portion of the growth cycle, it's important to choose a next step with the coach on what action they can take when it comes to their original goal. For example, what do more collaborative observations look like? The ultimate pursuit is to be more collaborative. As we know, Gavin chose the goal he wanted to work on through a coaching cycle, which was creating a more collaborative stakeholder group and changing the name to the Collaborative Leadership Team (CLT).

After reviewing and reflecting, Gavin knows the goal that he wants to work on with Michelle. He collects some evidence to bring to their meeting, knowing that he will have to collect more evidence as they go through the process.

GAVIN SEEKS ADVICE FROM A FRIEND

Gavin reflects on how he is moving forward with Michelle and her insights regarding Brad. Although he is glad he took the time to clear the air with Brad, he isn't sure it is enough. He feels that he needs to take some of these coaching techniques and philosophies and use them with Beth and Brad. After all, if coaching worked for him, why wouldn't it work for his assistant principals? He starts to understand that he needs to provide them with a different experience than he had when he was an assistant.

The night before, he emailed his friend Ken Lein. Ken is an experienced principal in Albany, New York. Gavin asks Ken for his advice on how to move forward with Brad and Beth. The following is Ken's response:

Hi Gavin,

Your question is a really good one, and something I had to think a lot about.

After twelve years as a principal, I had the opportunity to hire an assistant principal for the first time. I wanted someone who shared my core beliefs and vision. I did not want a lackey, but someone to work alongside me to realize that vision. At the interview, each candidate was asked how they saw the role of the assistant principal. All candidates gave acceptable answers, but one candidate, when given the opportunity to ask questions, asked me how I saw the role. Without much thought, I answered "a partnership." This collaborative approach has led to a trusting relationship, and while some roles are delineated, each of us crosses over outside any defined role to get the work done.

When I sat in my first principal's chair, I thought "Now what?" Despite the many doubts I had about my own efficacy, I still tried to do it all myself. One learns quickly that it is impossible to have sustained success without a collaborative approach. As a result, my coaching includes helping to build my assistant principal's self-efficacy, and teaching him the value of collective efficacy. I want him to be better prepared than I was when he takes on his own building.

I had a colleague ask me what day during the week I met with my assistant principal. That was a foreign concept. Accessibility matters. We chat before and after school almost every day, and have conversations throughout the day. We reflect on decisions together, both his and mine. I have never

(Continued)

(Continued)

felt the need to micro-manage because of this collaborative relationship. Besides ongoing conversation, my approach to coaching also includes two of Bandura's four sources of efficacy: performance accomplishments and vicarious experiences. My coaching uses both modeling (vicarious experience) and allowing for decision making (performance accomplishments).

My coaching began with modeling. Modeling took many forms: thinking aloud as we discussed the day before and after school, walking the building together and visiting classrooms, greeting students each morning at the front door, facilitating meetings then changing roles, and copies and blind copies on emails to parents, teachers, and cabinet members. This time together allowed for ongoing reflection and debriefing. While modeling never really ends, a time comes to release to strengths. In our case, it was the work he was doing with the change in school-wide behavior. He began facilitating the weekly Behavior Support Team meetings. He strengthened his efficacy through performance accomplishments (we got results) at the same time as we built the collective.

This meeting became an exemplar for collective efficacy. While I created the space for the collective, he has brought it forward. Two of the norms he suggested were everyone has a voice, and if you disagree, disagree with purpose. In other words, have reasons as to why you disagree and have a possible solution. At this meeting, agree or disagree, everyone's work is validated and appreciated.

My assistant principal will say the greatest coaching I do for him is trusting him to make decisions knowing that there will be no backlash if we misstep. He appreciates that we reflect together and move forward together. It seems to have worked in building efficacy and preparing him for his next stop.

I hope that helps.

Ken

Gavin respects Ken a great deal, and his email provides him with some direction in his desire to be the leader that both Beth and Brad need in order for them to reach their full potential as assistant principals who will one day have their own building to lead.

In the End

Over the month that Michelle and Gavin have been working together, Gavin has come around a bit to the coaching process. He begins talking openly about the coaching process with teachers, and Michelle notices that more and more of them say hi to her when she walks into the school. Some go as far as inviting her into the classroom if she "needs a break from coaching the boss," which she thinks is great because they are beginning to show their senses of humor.

Although many leaders say they would like to be coached, there are still leaders who are nervous about the process. It's interesting because leaders will say that instructional coaching is important for teachers, but those leaders suffer from the same insecurities that teachers do when they are first matched up with a coach.

In this chapter, Michelle discussed being OPEN to coaching, which meant taking the **opportunity** seriously, finding a **purpose** behind coaching, holding high **expectations** of the process, and looking for **next** steps. Walk-throughs are only one of the areas that we need to learn more about, because we need to make sure that the tools we use (i.e., walk-throughs, teacher observations, faculty meetings, impact teams, etc.) provide opportunities for dialogue and do not focus on one-sided monologue where the teachers are left feeling as though the process was done *to* them.

At the end of the chapter we know that Gavin has established a goal, but we are not sure what it is. All of our leadership actions need to lead to the greater good, which is working collectively to focus on student learning. If one of our initiatives does not lead to authentic learning experiences, it will chip away at our ultimate goal of working together collectively, because our actions will not be aligned with our goals. Figure 4.3 illustrates the idea of the interconnectedness of our actions.

To be successful, Gavin will need to understand that he cannot do it alone, because leaders do not have the self-efficacy

Figure 4.3   Ingredients for Successful Leadership

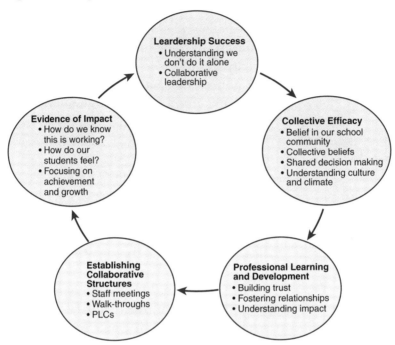

to be successful in every part of their role and need the collective efforts of staff. Leaders build collective efficacy through having a belief in their school community and collectively establishing goals that they can explore through professional learning and development. By not being the only one talking in professional learning and development sessions and encouraging others to have a voice, leaders match their actions with their beliefs that then carry over into their collaborative structures. Most importantly, however, they work together to collect evidence to understand their impact on student learning—student learning that focuses on growth and achievement.

Leaders like Gavin have to begin by focusing on one goal while understanding that those pieces and parts in between have an impact on that greater goal. Looking at leadership actions as a cycle will help keep that clear.

DISCUSSION QUESTIONS

Coaches and Leaders:

- What does OPEN to coaching mean to you?
- How do you work through being nervous about telling staff that you are working with a coach?
- How do you focus on one goal while not getting distracted by other issues that arise in your day-to-day actions?

Leaders:

- How can you foster more authentic walk-throughs?
- What is one area of leadership that you find frustrating because it builds compliance and not collective efficacy? What can you do to move toward more collective efficacy in that area?

Coaches:

- How do you help keep leaders focused?

TAKE ACTION

- Establish a goal that will have an impact on your school climate. It will help for you to understand your current reality.
- Look at your leadership tools, such as walk-through protocols. Do they inspire dialogue or one-sided monologue?
- Ask teachers through an anonymous survey how they feel about walk-throughs or the observation process. Ask them if walk-throughs have helped change the level of impact they have on their students.

GAVIN ESTABLISHES HIS GOAL

A s Gavin becomes more comfortable with Michelle, he begins to trust the coaching process. It is time to dive deeper into a goal that will have a larger impact on all staff. Gavin chooses a goal that could involve a great deal of learning and impact. However, too often the process that Gavin focuses on is about compliance and seat time.

Gavin chooses to create a building-level professional learning community (PLC). He feels he needs to look at PLCs because they were established in every school by Dr. Coppola, and during his visits to different PLCs within Naylor Middle School he found them to be lackluster. Teachers rarely discussed impact on learning and spent their time talking with Gavin about issues happening in the building. Sometimes it was rather ironic, because they spent their PLC time discussing how they needed more prep time to plan for their lessons. Gavin knows that those teachers who complained the most didn't see, or didn't want to see, the connection between their PLC and what they needed to do in the classroom.

Gavin wants a larger PLC at the building level because he feels that it would help model what the department PLCs should look like, and it would give him a chance to foster trust among a group of staff representative of the building that would hopefully spread out over the whole building. He is a believer in grassroots efforts and that by starting with smaller groups, he can establish trust in small pockets and position himself as the instructional leader he so badly wants to be in his principalship.

Since Gavin and Michelle's very first meeting, he has considered many different options, but he wants to work on something that is directly related to a district initiative. Gavin notices that his superintendent refers to the PLC process a lot, but no building has a PLC process, and his would be the first. He hopes that will set him apart so he can gain the confidence of Dr. Coppola. What he doesn't really understand is that he has her confidence; he just lacks confidence in himself.

Gavin's Collaborative Leadership Growth Cycle

Goal Setting—Gavin chose the building-level PLC process for many reasons. One reason is due to how much his superintendent cares about it, but he also chose it because he has heard countless conversations in the hallway from teachers who complain that they don't have time to keep up with changes and that morale is low. He believes the PLC process will help change that.

Current Reality—Gavin understands, mostly from anecdotal evidence, that only a few of the department PLCs are functioning effectively. PLCs are generally about seat time on the part of the teachers and building compliance as opposed to authentic learning. A building-level PLC would help model how the department PLCs should operate.

Evidence Gathering—Gavin is pondering how to collect evidence. Should he gather exit interviews after the building-level PLC, surveys, individual interviews, or all of the above? This is an area he needs to discuss with Michelle.

Action Step—Where should he start? Who would be interested in joining? What if no one wants to join?

Collaboration—The ultimate goal is for the members of building-level PLC to work collectively with one another and have an impact on student learning, which means gathering collective evidence to understand the impact they are having. One of the other goals is to make sure that the school leaders—Gavin, Brad, and Beth—all take part in the PLC process.

Gavin doesn't want to complicate the situation, but he also wants to be more collaborative with Beth and Brad because they are finally at the emerging stage of functioning like a team. Since his days with his former principal, Gavin has been concerned that he is doing to Beth and Brad what his former principal did to him, which was nothing more than hand out discipline duties and take on a bystander approach in the relationship. Now that Brad is more on board, Gavin wants to take this as an opportunity to use his coaching relationship with Michelle as a guide to coaching Beth and Brad.

In the first month that school was in session, Gavin would meet with Beth and Brad when they needed to, rather than set up scheduled meetings and focus on the learning happening in the building. He wants to make sure that he now offers them a much better and more collaborative leadership experience, and he is beginning to feel as if this is his chance to make his way out of being reactive and help him focus on being proactive. He believes the building-level PLC will be a great way to get people to come together and share ideas, but he knows it won't ever come together unless he initiates the idea.

"I want a building-level PLC to act as a model for how the department PLCs should be running," Gavin confides to Michelle. "I mean, in theory, I know we should focus on student learning, but I think it's a good place to begin establishing trust, and quite honestly, I'm a bit tired of people looking to me to solve all of their issues. I feel like I need to have a group where we can focus on those issues together," Gavin explains. What Gavin would soon realize is that if he went about this goal correctly, his confidence as a leader would grow as well.

"How will you measure your impact?" Michelle asks.

This is not an easy question to answer. Michelle introduces him to the concept of SMARTER goals. As she speaks, Gavin takes notes to help him understand how SMARTER goals can help him with his new building-level PLC goal.

Specific

Measureable

Achievable

Realistic

Timely

Evaluate

Reevaluate

Gavin and Michelle both know that Gavin can't answer this question without a great deal of thinking. They agree that he needs some time to determine who will be on the PLC and then the PLC together will establish a goal.

"What role will you, Beth, and Brad play in all of this?" Michelle asks.

"We could co-construct the protocols and make sure teachers are accountable for what we come up with?" Gavin asks more than tells.

"Part of the issue with leaders is that they expect teachers to collaborate, but they don't always take an active role in the collaboration, besides giving teachers one more thing to do," Michelle says. This makes Gavin a little uncomfortable.

"But isn't it my job to set the direction of the building?" he asks.

Michelle pauses for a moment before speaking. "I think what makes leadership so difficult sometimes is that leaders feel they have to set the direction, when really they have to give up some of the control and let the group set the direction. If they don't give up some of the control, they are not empowering teachers," Michelle answers.

Michelle also knows that Gavin could not have established the building-level PLC in the first weeks of his leadership because he was still establishing trust with his staff. Applying the Goldilocks principle (not too soon, not too late), Michelle knows that this is the right time for Gavin to move forward with this process.

Michelle helps Gavin understand that when leaders don't feel self-confident, they often try to control everyone so that the staff won't see that they are really just insecure. This is a very powerful moment for Gavin, because he realizes that what Michelle describes is exactly what was happening to him.

"Speaking of areas where you don't always feel confident—how has the lawsuit worked out so far?" Michelle asks.

"It's been a bit stressful. The director of special education, our school lawyer, the parents, and their lawyer met a few times. They have actually backed off on the lawsuit but we had to provide assurances that their daughter is getting the services she really needs. I mean we are at fault, so I feel like this could have gone the other way," Gavin explains.

"I'm glad that's working out," Michelle says.

"It was a good learning lesson," Gavin answers.

"Those situations usually are," Michelle responds.

WHY DOES COLLECTIVE EFFICACY STILL MATTER?

Michelle finds herself talking about collective efficacy quite a bit because it's such an effective way to address issues and grow as a school community. A few years ago, Michelle heard John Hattie speak at a conference where he announced that collective efficacy was the number one influence out of 251 influences that he had researched with a team at The University of Melbourne in Australia. Because of its incredibly high impact, Michelle began doing her own research on collective efficacy. She learned that collective efficacy has an effect size of 1.57. This is nearly quadruple the hinge point of .40,

Coach's Corner

Understand the Research You Promote

How often have you heard the term *research based?* Are you tired of hearing it? If you use the term in a conversation, are you sure you are using it correctly? Have you read the research or just merely looked at a summary?

Unfortunately, too many educators promote research-based strategies but do not understand how research is supposed to be used in the classroom.

For examples, we need go no further than when Carol Dweck recently clarified the growth mindset and Howard Gardner dispelled the myths around multiple intelligences. Additionally, it happens often with the Visible Learning work of John Hattie, who is a leading researcher in the field of education.

Visible learning is about making learning visible for students through the use of learning intentions and success criteria. It is founded on deep research around meta-analysis, which is a mathematical approach to combine many large studies, the veracity of which relies on effect sizes.

Many of my posts on the *Finding Common Ground* blog have focused on John Hattie and his visible learning research. This is not meant to be a plug for Hattie's work, nor for mine; it's just that I've come across a troubling trend when I speak to school and district leaders about his research. They look at the influences with the highest effect sizes and then dictate that teachers should use those, without understanding how each influence looks in action nor the research behind it.

The power of Hattie's research is that he brings so many studies together and therefore can show how much of an impact specific influences can have on learning. However, that is where issues begin to arise, not for Hattie's work but rather how it is interpreted and then used by school and district leaders and teachers. And it serves as a cautionary tale.

To avoid the pitfalls of misusing research, there are three areas that leaders should examine before they ever bring another "research-based" initiative to their schools:

1. **Don't focus too much on the numbers.**

   In educational research, a .40 effect size typically refers to a year's worth of growth for a year's input. Hattie refers to this .40 as the hinge point (e.g., Hattie 2012a, 2012b). All of his 251 influences have an effect size attached to them. Some of the influences are well above .40, and many of them are well below .40. There are leaders who believe that their teachers should only focus on influences that are above .40, and some suggest that their teachers should only focus on those above .60. After all, the larger the effect size, the bigger the impact. Unfortunately, this is flawed thinking, because it's not always about the effect size but how we use the influence. It is the story about how the influences overlap that matters, and this is why Hattie called his model of overlap Visible Learning. Educators need to look at more than just larger effect sizes.

2. **The shiny new toy isn't for everyone . . . especially if you use it incorrectly.**

Too often leaders, whether or not they use Hattie's research, chase after the shiny new toy that everyone is talking about, or they use whatever new research-based solution is currently in vogue, because they assume it's going to revolutionize their schools. Unfortunately, they implement the shiny new toy incorrectly, and it results in no revolutionary change. To implement anything properly, we must understand our current reality or the new toy will never work. We shouldn't chase after new toys because they look good on the shelf; we should chase after them because we need them and know how to use them.

When it comes to Hattie's research—or any other educational research for that matter—it's about helping educators understand what works best for them at that moment in time and making sure we all have a common understanding of how that particular influence should be implemented. After all, we may choose an intervention with a larger effect size and implement it poorly.

3. **Leaders need not be all show and no go.**

Leaders tend to call out which influence might work best based on their gut feeling, but very few have read the research deeply enough to learn how those influences should work. Regardless of whether or not the influence has a large effect size, it's important to understand what the research says. This, however, also means that leaders have to focus on implementing a small number of influences for an extended period as opposed to touting their favorite influence of the week.

If leaders are going to position themselves as the lead learners who dictate what works best, they should have an understanding of what they dictate before they dictate it.

which equates to a year's worth of student growth for a year's schooling. During her research, Michelle kept in mind that as a leader and a coach, she needed to understand the nuances of a theory or practice at a deep level before introducing only the surface-level aspect of it to staff or coachees.

The nuance of collective efficacy is that to maximize its effect, we have to have a protocol in place for the structures we use (e.g., PLC), we have to focus on a problem of practice, and we have to feed that problem of practice with evidence that teachers trust (T. Guskey, personal communication, May 8, 2017). Additionally, teachers have to see evidence that what they are doing is having an impact on student learning, and they need to keep feeding the process with that evidence. This is something that Gavin knows now because of his conversations with Michelle, which also illustrates why establishing a goal with a coach can sometimes take a back seat to fostering trust and learning other, more important baseline information, like self-efficacy and collective efficacy, first.

Coach's Corner

Raise Self-Efficacy

- Have a protocol in place (e.g., PLC, faculty meeting, teacher observation process, data teams, impact teams, etc.).
- Use evidence you trust (e.g., locally developed measures, student feedback, curriculum-based measures, etc.).
- See improvement in learning within weeks, not months.

Over the course of their relationship, Michelle will help Gavin understand that collective efficacy is helpful to him as well, because he does not feel efficacious in all of his leadership situations, and working with teachers collectively will help raise his feeling of efficacy in certain situations. Collective efficacy has the potential to help raise the efficacy of those in the group.

Michelle understands that what makes leadership coaching so complicated is that there is a specific goal that Gavin needs to work on with her, but he also has priorities that he needs to focus on as a principal. It's important to think of the goal with a leadership coach as a small thread of principal voice spreading out over time.

By working with Michelle on one goal, it helps Gavin build momentum, and he can use what he learns through coaching on those other pieces of the much bigger leadership puzzle. Michelle likes to look at coaching as a grassroots effort to help leaders get their feet under them, and then they can use the skills they learn in other facets of their job. It is something she sees happening with Gavin, especially when it comes to his assistant principal, Beth.

Coach's Corner

Assess Your Own Style of Coaching

- If you are a leader, what goal do you think is important for assistant principals to work on?
- In your experience, what should assistant principals focus on to become better leaders?
- If you have assistants, are you honest with them about their areas of strength and weakness?

The Story of Beth Lopez

Beth Lopez had been a school counselor for many years. She and Gavin knew each other really well. Beth didn't apply for the job as principal when Principal Alan Johnson retired because she had only been in the role of assistant for two years, and she wanted more time to acclimate to leadership. Her role as a counselor typically involved helping teachers, students, and families get through struggles. There were times when teachers approached her about testing and paper trails but she usually found a way to be more collaborative with colleagues, and she was respected for asking insightful questions of teachers who were looking for an easy way out with students they deemed too tough for their classroom.

Beth was actually the one who called Gavin to tell him about the job opening and encouraged him to apply. She liked working with him in their regional circles and thought he had what it takes to take over Naylor Middle School. Secretly she thought the building needed someone from the outside because Alan was often toxic, and she was concerned that both she and Brad would be seen as furthering the lack of leadership that Alan established. She noticed Brad becoming less engaging with staff and students, and he could be heard talking negatively about the frequent flyers, which is what he called students who were referred to him repeatedly.

Beth usually opted for the counseling strategy with students she saw for disciplinary reasons, but Brad was quick to suspend. Alan never questioned either of their styles, and he even seemed to match Beth up with students he wanted to give another chance to, as opposed to students he thought didn't belong in school (who he assigned to Brad), which is why he took control over reading the referrals before giving them out to each assistant to take care of the next day.

Beth was a bit worried about Gavin, however. His personality seemed to change a bit over the first few weeks after the students arrived. During the summer, he was collaborative with her, but as the year began, he seemed to try to control everything. She saw Michelle Hebert enter the building twice and remembered when Michelle had coached a few of the other leaders Beth had become friends with in regional meetings. Michelle had an excellent reputation, and Beth was hopeful that she would have an impact on Gavin's leadership. However, she never said anything to Gavin about seeing Michelle, because she wanted to wait until Gavin was comfortable enough to tell her on his own. Beth was happy when Gavin called to tell her about being coached, and she was equally happy when he told her that he had spoken to Brad as well. Beth felt like their administrative team was finally moving in the right direction.

//

FOUR PRIORITIES OF LEADERSHIP

Michelle understands that there are four priorities leaders face in their role: student and community engagement, communication, collective efficacy (purposeful collaboration among different groups), and the political climate (district, state, and national).

These four priorities came up in a small-scale study of school leaders that Michelle had read recently. If these are the priorities that leaders would like to work on with a coach, it's important to get a proper understanding of each and then talk about how coaches can help leaders work on them.

Clearly, each one of these priorities can blend into another depending on the situation. For example, Gavin chose a building-level PLC. PLCs are all about collective efficacy. If each member of the PLC does not believe in each other, they will not get to the deep learning necessary to improve student learning. However, it's even a bit more important than that. A building-level PLC, when done correctly, can take on all four of the priorities, which will strengthen the school community. Figure 5.1 illustrates how this happens.

Michelle knows that there are times when the priorities are set for principals because central office administration provides them with the direction, directly (you are coming in because I need you to change this) or indirectly (Gavin choosing building-level PLCs because it's important but also because it's a structure his superintendent brought in), upon

Figure 5.1   PLCs and the Four Priorities

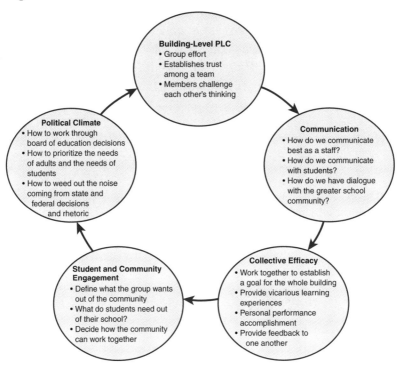

hiring them for the job. Michelle understands that other times leaders walk into a situation and have to begin looking at what needs to be addressed. They have time to sit back and observe before making changes.

Gavin began his principalship with a deficit mindset. He walked into the situation wondering what needed fixing and how he could help make the building better. However, his insecurities got the best of him from time to time, which is why Michelle is playing an important part in his here and now. Michelle understands that many leaders focus on how fortunate they are to be in a certain school district because of an outstanding school community, engaging teaching and learning, or an innovative building structure, but she knows it's also human nature to wonder what needs to be improved and how the leader can improve it. Gavin seems to have found the sweet spot to help him focus on where he fits in through establishing a more authentic and collaborative building-level PLC.

IN THE END

Coaching can feel like taking two steps forward and one step back. In Gavin's case, he is beginning to feel a bit more trust toward Michelle and therefore becoming OPEN to coaching. It's hard for a leader to accept being coached. When leaders find themselves working with a coach, they have a few insecurities to work through before they can really get to the heart of focusing on a goal.

Gavin needs to take the time to tell staff that he is working with Michelle. It's important for Gavin to tell the staff formally, because it sets the tone for the school and lets teachers know that being in a coaching relationship is a positive way of approaching our own personal and professional growth.

More importantly, Gavin has established the goal that he wants to create a building stakeholder group or PLC. Although Gavin is the one who established the goal, the goal itself will lead to stronger teacher voice and input if it is done correctly. Gavin, in turn, approached Beth and Brad about creating goals for themselves that would benefit the school.

Beth chose to focus on engaging the school's minoritized populations. Brad chose to focus on the increase in suspensions he was responsible for providing. The suspension conversation between Brad and Gavin was not an easy one, but Brad saw a clear difference in the number of suspensions he had versus the number that Beth had. He knew he had to approach discipline differently.

Coaches are often told that leaders cannot wait to work with us, and then when we get into the situation we realize that some of the leaders want to work with us, while others want nothing to do with us. Those leaders were "voluntold" to be coached. That's OK, because the onus is on the coach to prove himself or herself with the leader. After all, leaders are busy and they need to see that the coach they are working with can offer them something of value. As a coach, if you can't offer something valuable, get out. Leaders are too busy to waste their time on ineffective coaching, and the coach really needs to understand that every moment with the leader is a valuable moment. That's the mindset that Michelle has going into every meeting with Gavin.

DISCUSSION QUESTIONS

Coaches and Leaders:

- Where do you feel most self-confident?
- Where do you feel least self-confident?
- What did you learn from the Coach's Corner on understanding the research we promote?
- Do you use SMARTER goals? In what way do you use them? How effective are they?

Leaders:

- Out of the four priorities, which one is most important to you?

  ○ Which one offers more of a challenge?

  ○ How do you approach that challenge?

- What area do you think is most important for assistant principals to work on?
- How do you build collective efficacy among staff?

Coaches:

- When it comes to goal setting, is there another way Michelle should have approached the situation?

TAKE ACTION

- Change your mindset. Challenges are an opportunity to learn.
- Check on your PLCs. Are they focusing on learning and impact?
- Create a building-level stakeholder group.
  - Make sure that you have co-chairs and do not run the meeting.
  - Make sure people feel as though they have a place at the table and their voice is valued.

6

A SURVEY THAT INSPIRES COLLABORATION

As a school principal I built collective efficacy without understanding that I was building collective efficacy. Sometimes we get so caught up in the terms, and feel as though we don't always know where to start, that we don't realize we were doing it all along.

Truthfully, I didn't have a choice but to build efficacy among staff. It was a necessity because I did not have an assistant principal, and we needed to come together as a staff in order to grow as a school community. Sometimes we had to focus on tragic events, while other times we were able to focus on learning.

One of the things I'm most proud of as a leader is how we came together as a staff during our Principal's Advisory Council (PAC). PAC involved stakeholders from each grade level and special area, and it was where I began to get the idea to flip faculty meetings. It was also where we got into some heated debates about schooling. And it was where we came together because the rhetoric in New York State, where I was a principal, was not kind to teachers and public schools.

The staff I had the opportunity to lead and learn from inspired me to speak out against high-stakes testing being tied to teacher evaluation and supported me when I spoke out through my *Education Week* blog about how state assessments provide us with a great deal of stress but not a lot of feedback on how students are learning. They also supported me when the district office seemed to share my frustrations behind closed doors but did little to speak out about it publicly.

Don't get me wrong, we were not perfect, and PAC was not always a meeting I wanted to go to because there were other priorities that I needed to deal with when PAC was taking place. However, it became the venue we needed to discuss our frustrations and do something about them.

One of the things you will notice about Gavin is that he becomes vulnerable with staff in this chapter. As you read all of this you will probably wonder whether I am Gavin or Michelle Hebert. I will let you move on with that question in your mind. One of the things I hope you gain from this chapter is the importance of being vulnerable as a leader. Many leaders believe that makes us weak, but I believe being vulnerable makes us stronger.

After Gavin had been working with Michelle for a few months, he sent an email to staff asking for a volunteer to take a stakeholder position on the Collaborative Leadership Team (CLT). In his email, he promised that group members would have authentic voices and be able to supply more than input; they would set the course for improving building morale and student learning. Based on their Annual Professional Performance Review (APPR), staff members had to each set a goal for the year that they would collect evidence on, and CLT could be that goal for one member of each department and special area in the school.

Before sending the email, Gavin takes a deep breath, looks at it one more time, and presses *send*. He has been working with Michelle on being more vulnerable, and this is about as vulnerable as he has ever been. He hopes that his actions won't work against him. Here is Gavin's email:

Hi Everyone,

I hope this finds you well. Please excuse what will no doubt be a longer email than usual.

Over our first two months of school, I have had many conversations with you individually and as a group about school morale. I know this is not a new topic for us to discuss, but I do worry about the impact it has on student learning, and our happiness when coming into school every day. I would like us to work on this together.

As you know I taught for 10 years before I went into school leadership, so I understand all too well that shared decision making really means "you are all fine just as long as you share in the decision I am making," and I would like to change that.

I would like for us to create a Collaborative Leadership Team (CLT) together. Although my actions over the first month of school haven't always shown I love collaboration, I would like you to help me change that. I am looking for at least one member per department and special area to use their goal setting per APPR and join CLT.

A few weeks ago, I sent out a Google survey around teacher voice, and the following are some of the narratives that you used to answer the question on what you want out of our school community.

"I want teachers to have more of a voice in the process."

"I feel like it's teachers against administration during the BLT meetings. They seem a bit defensive."

"I'd like more time to learn with my colleagues."

"I feel like our school is going in so many different directions that I'm lost."

"I want more time with my students and less time in meetings."

"I'd like for us to find more ways to meet the needs of our students. I don't think we're doing as good of a job as some of us think we're doing."

It is not lost on me that only around 50% of you filled out the survey, which means you didn't feel you had enough of a voice to take the time to fill it out because you feared that I wouldn't do anything with the results. I believe the CLT, which is really just a building-level PLC, is the way to do that.

(Continued)

(Continued)

Please let me know if you would like to join us for our first meeting on Monday at 2:45.

Thank you for your time.

Gavin

Within about twenty minutes he hears from two people to say they will join. As he looks at his calendar, he realizes those two people, Maggie and Sanjay, are each finishing up their grade-level meeting. After their emails, there is silence on this topic for about two days. Gavin is getting nervous.

On Friday afternoon, Gavin hears from about eight more teachers. He has images in his head of teachers meeting up and discussing what CLT would mean and drawing the short straws or colleagues putting their fingers on their noses and saying, "*Not it!*" In reality, some of those exact conversations did take place.

In a Word document, Gavin makes a list of the people who will be joining the CLT:

Isabella: 6th- and 7th-grade science

Brian: 7th- and 8th-grade social studies

Traesyn: PE

Sanjay: 6th-grade social studies, 7th-grade ELA

Janelle: 7th- and 8th-grade ELA

Linda: 6th- and 7th-grade math

Anika: 6th-, 7th-, and 8th-grade self-contained special education

Jaylese: School counselor

Cherise: Academic intervention specialist

Jasmine: School nurse

Brad and Beth: Assistant principals

Beth tells Gavin that the influx of volunteers is due to the union meeting—yes, the union meeting. On Friday mornings from 7:00 to 7:30, Gavin meets with the two building representatives for the union. It is one of the things he learned to do from his previous experience as an assistant principal. While he was a teacher, the teacher's union wasn't his favorite group because it seemed to focus on adult issues, such as teachers who don't get along or prep time, when we should be spending our time focusing on student learning. However, he thinks that the union at Naylor Middle School is a bit more positive. Gavin appreciates that group members perform community outreach and focus on the needs of students. He wants to create open communication, so they choose Friday mornings as the best time to meet.

Anika and Janelle, his union reps, tell him that people are nervous about joining the CLT, and he assures them that he wants an authentic PLC/shared decision-making process, because the results of a survey he sent out asking what teachers want from Naylor Middle School seem to point to a CLT as the best entry point to address the issues raised. A few of the teachers also tell Beth that conversations are taking place regarding the CLT. Gavin, Beth, and Brad talk about how one email or conversation can have a ripple effect through a building, which is exactly what happened from the conversation Gavin had with Anika and Janelle. A mere few hours later, Gavin suddenly has more volunteers for the CLT. This is not a coincidence.

THE SURVEY THAT INSPIRED IT ALL

Gavin has definitely become more open to coaching over the first few months of working with Michelle. He has realized that he is not the only leader in the world who suffers from insecurities. He has even taken some time to rejoin the Voxer group of leaders that he had been missing from since the beginning of the year. He spoke to Kyle O'Brien, the moderator of the group, and Kyle was completely understanding of Gavin's need to leave the virtual PLN that communicated through the walkie-talkie app, so he added him back to the group.

Gavin mostly listens to the messages others in the group have left while he commutes to work. Occasionally, he listens while at the gym. One of the ideas he picks up from Kyle is conducting a survey with staff that focuses on his leadership skills. Gavin is beyond nervous to see what his teachers think of him, but he asks Kyle for a copy so he can send it to the staff. The survey also focuses on what school staff want out of their experience as teachers and staff at Naylor Middle School. Michelle wants Gavin to be more vulnerable, and this is about as vulnerable as he can get.

The anonymous survey asked one question: *"What is one thing you would like to improve about the leadership at Naylor Middle School?"* Gavin sends out the survey with an explanation that he wants to get some baseline information on how to move forward as a building. Out of 62 teachers and 37 staff members, 49 people filled out the survey and provided the following answers:

"I want teachers to have more of a voice in the building."

"Administration seems disconnected from teachers."

"Administration sometimes seems to care about parents more than they care about teachers."

"Morale is low."

"I feel like it's teachers against administration during the faculty meetings. Administration seems a bit defensive."

"I'd like more time to learn from my colleagues."

"I feel supported by my leaders."

"Uninterrupted prep time."

"More supportive parents."

"I like that the administrators come into my classroom."

"I like that my administrator leaves me alone so I can teach."

"I think Gavin, Brad and Beth really care about us as teachers."

"I like how the leaders know the names of students."

"I feel like our school is going in so many different directions that I'm lost."

"I want more time with my students and less time in meetings."

"I'd like for us to find more ways to meet the needs of our students. I don't think we're doing as good of a job as some of us think we're doing."

"I just wish administration would tell us what they want us to do."

"We have a morale issue and no one seems to want to do anything about it."

"I feel really fortunate to be a part of this school."

Gavin is neither broken by frustration nor surprised by the answers. It doesn't escape him that only one comment focused on students, while all of the others focused on teachers or parents. This is an issue that many schools face, and he wants to change the dialogue to learning.

Brad points out that the percentage of those teachers and staff who filled it out the survey is telling. Around 50% is good for researchers but not for a school principal surveying the staff. However, Brad follows up by saying that Gavin's predecessor never conducted surveys, so this is all new to staff.

"I think it was a really good first effort," Brad says. "We'll get there with staff, but they haven't experienced this before."

"We just need to prove that we will do something about the feedback on the surveys," Beth says. "After we prove that we are listening, more staff will come on board."

Gavin appreciates the support from Brad and Beth. He knows they have some deep trust issues to deal with, even though on the surface, things are going better. Gavin also knows that he has to get to the root cause of these issues, or things will not improve at the magnitude they can.

What Gavin knows about what he read in the surveys is that these answers could be the catalyst for a building-level stakeholder group. He also knows it is no longer his job to carry all of this on his shoulders, and that is what he tells Janelle and Anika at their weekly meeting. Now, he has the volunteers and the meeting is set for the following week. The ball is in his court to prove he wants to know the collective thoughts of others.

Coach's Corner

Collaborative Leadership Team (CLT)

- Set parameters for the group.
  - Who are the co-chairs?
  - What are the responsibilities of each member?
  - Who sets the course the group takes?
  - How often will group members meet as a team?

- As principal, talk less than the other members of the group. Every time the leader talks, it will seem as though it is his or her meeting.
- Those not on the CLT will question CLT members, so be prepared. Establish how CLT members should respond when colleagues confront them about the direction CLT is taking.

THE MORNING AFTER

The morning after the initial CLT meeting, Janelle and Anika, the union reps for the building, are elected as co-chairs by the other members of the CLT. Apparently, that morning they met because they wanted to define teacher leadership for the group, and they went directly to Gavin to inform him about their democratic process that resulted in their newfound leadership positions on the committee. Janelle and Anika are not afraid to speak their minds, which Gavin only sees as a plus in the whole situation because he already has a regularly scheduled meeting with them on Friday mornings. Bringing in the co-chair model for the cabinet, especially two people who also happen to be the building representatives for the union, is an important step; it shows that Gavin wants to work with them and not against them.

Anika, Janelle, Beth, Brad, and Gavin agree that the next CLT meeting will focus on the following protocols:

- Mutually agreed upon as the focus of CLT:

  - Use a SMARTER goal to measure it.

- Everyone contributes.
- Every meeting ends with an action plan, which may include:

  - CLT members going back to talk with their grade-level or department colleagues to disseminate information.
  - CLT members being responsible for finding evidence, research, or resources.

- It is OK to challenge the beliefs of others as long as it is done respectfully.
- The focus will be on student learning and not adult issues.
- We may not get all of what we want, but we will have a voice in the process and get a piece of what we want.

Although Gavin knows he can't let go of his status as principal, he doesn't want to be considered the smartest or most important voice in the room. No one is as important as all of them. Over the first few meetings over two months, the CLT process starts to become more authentic.

During that time frame, Gavin feels fortunate because of the progress they are making, and Michelle calls him to discuss what he has been able to do in the CLT meetings. Excitement in the CLT process is growing, but they still have the cold, dark, winter months to get through. That is a time when teachers are often overwhelmed; the holidays cause students to become distracted, and the weather does not always cooperate for them to go outside and get fresh air at recess. All of this plays a part in how people function from day to day.

Coach's Corner

Create a Collaborative Leadership Team (CLT)

- Choose a teacher or staff member from each grade level, team, or department.
- Select representatives from special areas, such as school social workers, psychologists, special education teachers, and teacher's aides.
- The purpose of the CLT should be to choose a goal that will help focus on learning, for example:

  o Faculty meetings that are professional development sessions
  o Walk-throughs and the feedback teachers receive
  o School climate—how to foster a more inclusive and supportive school climate
  o Learner dispositions—what dispositions all students should learn that will help them know where they are, how they are doing, and where to go next in their learning

- Someone on the CLT should be the notetaker, and those notes should be sent out to the faculty to keep a level of transparency.
- Stakeholders should report back to their individual teams to keep the goals and lines of communication open.
- The school leader should not lead the CLT. Choose two co-chairs to run the meeting.

COLLABORATIVE LEADERSHIP TEAM

During the first few CLT meetings, there were members who showed up but didn't say much. At other times, when their colleagues found them in the hallway and wanted to discuss the direction of the CLT, members of the group didn't always know what to say.

Anika and Janelle begin talking about possible goals for the CLT. Janelle likes when Gavin randomly selects students for the student focus groups and shares their interviews at the faculty meeting. However, she explains to Gavin that she and a few of her colleagues think something is missing because they never do anything with the information afterward. Gavin does not confide in them that he initially planned to use that information as a way to shame teachers, but he does say that he had an idea that didn't work out. The group talks about how the student focus groups might be a good place to begin, because it will also tie up a loose end for those teachers who feel like they are left hanging. However, Sanjay and Jaylese voice their concern about asking students for feedback. After all, it is just the student's perspective and they might have something to get back at a teacher for, so they might lie in the focus group.

"If a student is going to lie about a teacher, I believe that may be a big sign that we have an issue in the building," Brad says. "And as far as it being the student's perspective—absolutely! I mean, Gavin asked for your perspective in the survey he sent out to all of you. Does that make it less important to Gavin because it's just your perspective?" Brad asks.

Jaylese is visibly upset over Brad's response, but Sanjay nods his head in agreement. He realizes that Brad has raised a very valid point. After some time, they talk through the following:

Focus—Ask student focus groups, "What makes a good learner?" This has the potential of opening up Pandora's box on how students have changed and how they are coddled, but CLT members think maybe it is time to go there.

After they define their focus, Gavin brings the discussion around to SMARTER goals, which many of the teachers have heard of but never used.

Specific—What does good learning look like? Meaning, how do we actively engage students?

Measureable—Define authentic engagement with staff. During walk-throughs and formal classroom observations, Gavin, instructional coaches, and the walk-through team can use seating charts to highlight which students are actively engaged and which are not.

Assignable—Using the research of George T. Doran (1981), the team focuses on who is responsible for carrying out this goal.

Relevant—All students should be actively engaged in learning. This is a very relevant goal.

Timely—The first phase of this goal is to use faculty meetings to discuss staff understanding of authentic engagement and what strategies seem to work best with students. Phase two will involve Beth's goal, which is how to engage minoritized populations. Much of this discussion will take place next year.

Evaluate—At the end of the school year, Gavin would once again conduct student focus groups to evaluate their impact on what makes a good learner a good learner.

Reevaluate—At the beginning of next year, Gavin and the team would conduct student focus groups, but the CLT would look at the possibility of instituting learner dispositions in the school.

Over the trials and tribulations of the CLT and the daily interactions for a school leader, Michelle definitely sees growth in both Gavin's leadership and also in how he approaches the coaching relationship. In the months they worked together, Michelle saw the learning they did together go from a surface level, where Gavin just listened and didn't respond much, to a deep level, where he listened and responded with a greater understanding of how it relates to other parts of his leadership. As staff got a bit rougher around the edges because they were tired from the winter, Gavin dug deeper to find ways to inspire them.

Michelle knows that she has a defined period of time with Gavin and wants to continue to see him go from surface- to deep- to transfer-level learning, where he takes what they talk about and uses it in his practices (see Figure 6.1).

Gavin did indeed use some of Michelle's techniques with Beth, Brad, and the CLT. He found himself sitting back and asking questions more often and dominating the

Figure 6.1   Surface to Deep to Transfer Learning for Leaders

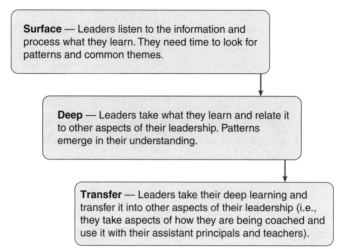

conversations a lot less. This was a big win for Michelle's coaching, because she saw Gavin empowering those around him as opposed to enabling them. However, he was not out of the woods yet as a leader.

As much as the CLT and his relationships with the stakeholders in the school community were moving in a positive direction, Michelle understands that Gavin is still a new leader. Yes, he has experience as an assistant, and he is doing an amazing job as a principal, but there will be more times when he hits the implementation dip and runs into roadblocks. Inexperienced leaders often revert back to old habits where they take control of the situation and give orders instead of take feedback. Working with others is hard. After all, most people get into teaching because they want to work with students or love a subject. They do not get into teaching because they want to work with other adults. All of this adult strife can have an impact on how leaders like Gavin collaborate with staff, and it certainly has an impact on his self-efficacy as a leader.

It's important for leaders to seek feedback to help them grow (Witherspoon, 2014). Unfortunately, due to a lack of training, politics in the job and in education, mandates that are both funded and unfunded, and district initiatives that are difficult to understand, leaders often find themselves spending their days focusing on tasks as opposed to student learning. This doesn't provide them with the opportunity to seek the feedback they need and deserve.

In the case of Gavin and Michelle, they communicated often so Michelle could provide the coaching feedback he needed. They did not wait for the face-to-face meetings because there were times the meetings were weeks apart, so they would talk via email or participate in a Zoom meeting so they could talk virtually. This communication was set up in the spirit of the Goldilocks principle—not too often, not too seldom, but just enough.

Coach's Corner

Strategies to Overcome the Challenges of Distance

Coaching relationships have their challenges, whether you're being coached by a leadership coach or are part of a critical friendship with someone within or outside the district. The greatest challenges have to do with time and proximity. The following items are important to remember when coaching:

- Regularly check in via phone calls and emails.
- Make the moments count when the coach and leader are together. Have an agenda set up to keep the meetings focused.
- Use social meeting tools like Zoom, Skype, or Google Hangouts. They are free services and will provide a face-to-face meeting when coaches can't be there in person.

SURFACE TO DEEP

To really go deep enough with the CLT, and in other parts of his leadership, Michelle understands that Gavin has to look inward before he can grow more as a leader, which he has done well over the last few months. Via email, Michelle reminds Gavin that she is going to send him a reflection questionnaire:

Hi Gavin,

I hope you are doing well.

I have to tell you that I am so proud of your growth as a leader over the last few months we have worked together. As we discussed, to keep that growth going, I thought I would send you this self-efficacy questionnaire that I came across recently. Remember that this is a tool for you to reflect on your leadership practices. Like we discussed before, I wanted to wait for you to do this until you had a few months of this principalship under your belt.

Please take some time to fill it out. It's best to do this before the school day or at the end of the day. We will go through your answers together at our next meeting.

See you soon!

Michelle

Gavin opens the email attachment and takes a look. *"Wow,"* he thinks to himself. He suddenly realizes that he sent teachers a survey asking what they want out of their school, but he had not done a self-reflection on what he wanted out of his leadership. Gavin decides to wait and work on the survey over the weekend. He isn't sure whether he should fill it out after coffee or red wine...

Principals' Self-Efficacy Questionnaire

The following questions ask about your perceptions of your ability to perform various tasks, such as curriculum management, management of teaching and learning, budgeting, management of the external environment, and school improvement planning. You are asked to make a judgment about your ability to perform each of the tasks in order to secure a successful resolution of the situation. Where possible, assume the situation applies to your present school setting.

(Continued)

(Continued)

It is recognized that principals may well feel different levels of confidence in their abilities, according to the nature of the task or problem, and therefore variations on the confidence scale may be expected.

Indicate your degree of confidence by circling the appropriate point on the 0 to 10 CONFIDENCE scale, based on the following question:

How confident can you be of securing a successful resolution of this situation?

SCHOOL IMPROVEMENT PLANNING

1. A small, yet influential and articulate group of staff members actively resists all attempts to implement the school's agreed priorities.

0	1	2	3	4	5	6	7	8	9	10

Totally Unconfident	Moderately Confident	Totally Confident

2. After much careful deliberation and due process your school has arrived at the point where two of its three priorities for the school improvement plan next year have been decided. However, the staff and parents are split equally in planning staff development initiatives. The teachers want all staff development funding to be spent on reading initiatives, and the parents want staff development funds spread evenly across the areas of reading, math, and science.

0	1	2	3	4	5	6	7	8	9	10

Totally Unconfident	Moderately Confident	Totally Confident

Indicate your degree of confidence by circling the appropriate point on the 0 to 10 CONFIDENCE scale, based on the following question:

How confident can you be of securing a successful resolution of this situation?

TEACHING, LEARNING, AND CURRICULUM

3. As principal, you, together with the teaching staff, have decided to introduce more peer tutoring and cooperative small group student learning across the school. Many parents are strongly opposed to this idea.

0	1	2	3	4	5	6	7	8	9	10

Totally   Moderately   Totally
Unconfident   Confident   Confident

4. You have decided that, after careful consideration, the students in your school would benefit from the introduction of an integrated curriculum, with team teaching and problem-based learning. A number of staff argue that these changes were debated years ago and they failed then, so why should they succeed this time?

0	1	2	3	4	5	6	7	8	9	10

Totally   Moderately   Totally
Unconfident   Confident   Confident

MANAGING STAFF

5. A female teacher has accused the male school resource officer (SRO) of sexual harassment. She wishes to register a formal complaint to you, as principal.

0	1	2	3	4	5	6	7	8	9	10

Totally   Moderately   Totally
Unconfident   Confident   Confident

6. As the newly appointed principal arriving at school, you note that all teaching staff have been at the school for a long period of time and the only change in staff has been your appointment as principal. You realize the staff is in the "comfort zone" and standards of achievement are low. After six months of reasoning and applying subtle pressure, a staff meeting is arranged to "have it out."

0	1	2	3	4	5	6	7	8	9	10

Totally   Moderately   Totally
Unconfident   Confident   Confident

Indicate your degree of confidence by circling the appropriate point on the 0 to 10 CONFIDENCE scale, based on the following question:

(Continued)

(Continued)

How confident can you be of securing a successful resolution to this situation?

BUDGETING

7. A minority group within the school (ESE students) has been identified as having a legitimate need for new equipment for adaptive physical education. The ESE teacher is well organized and motivated. He is able to obtain a grant from a professional sports franchise but needs an additional $8,000 from the school. Without consulting the principal, he negotiates with a local businessman who promises half of the money if the school will contribute the other half. There is sufficient money within the school budget, but the school finance committee feels strongly that too much money will be spent on a very small number of students. You have to guide the committee through the problem of weighing the needs of the minority against those of the majority, as finances are tight.

0	1	2	3	4	5	6	7	8	9	10

Totally Unconfident	Moderately Confident	Totally Confident

8. An examination of budgetary spending in midyear reveals the school is overspending across most of its budget categories. Approximately one half of the school would support cutbacks in expenditures, while the other half would not. Instead, they urge further income generation, through sponsorships and fundraising.

0	1	2	3	4	5	6	7	8	9	10

Totally Unconfident	Moderately Confident	Totally Confident

MANAGING PARENTS

9. A group of parents has openly canvassed other parents not to enroll children in the school because of a particular staff member. This has caused conflict between school and community. The union has backed the teacher, who is due to return from leave. The community is openly aggressive towards the teacher's return.

| 0 | 1 | 2 | 3 | 4 | 5 | 6 | 7 | 8 | 9 | 10 |

Totally
Unconfident

Moderately
Confident

Totally
Confident

Indicate your degree of confidence by circling the appropriate point on the 0 to 10 CONFIDENCE scale, based on the following question:

How confident can you be of securing a successful resolution to this situation?

10. A talented, highly motivated music teacher has been appointed to the school. She has made a distinct change to the teaching of music. Students are receiving an enlightened and rewarding program, and "good things" are happening in music for the first time in years. You have acknowledged these improvements by congratulating the teacher. You then receive phone calls and letters from irate parents who are most disturbed to discover that one of the music classes has been exposed to obscenities in the music recordings. The parents plan to take matters further, complaining to the district office and the media.

| 0 | 1 | 2 | 3 | 4 | 5 | 6 | 7 | 8 | 9 | 10 |

Totally
Unconfident

Moderately
Confident

Totally
Confident

MANAGING THE ENVIRONMENT

11. A union directive has asked staff to march in protest against asbestos-related issues. The district has declared that short-term leave may not be granted to staff intending to take part. Some staff have already indicated their intention to march but not to declare this on their leave form.

| 0 | 1 | 2 | 3 | 4 | 5 | 6 | 7 | 8 | 9 | 10 |

Totally
Unconfident

Moderately
Confident

Totally
Confident

12. A male teacher on your staff has a propensity to hit disruptive students. A journalist telephones you after having been contacted by

(Continued)

(Continued)

a parent whose child claims physical abuse by the teacher. The journalist is earnestly seeking the full story for inclusion in the next issue of the local newspaper.

0	1	2	3	4	5	6	7	8	9	10

Totally Unconfident	Moderately Confident	Totally Confident

Developed by Clive Dimmock, PhD, University of Western Australia, and John Hattie, PhD, University of Auckland, New Zealand. Permission granted to use the Principals' Self-Efficacy Questionnaire by John Hattie.

In the End

On Saturday, Gavin pours himself a glass of red wine and sits down to fill out the questionnaire. The questions about curriculum, budgeting, and managing the environment are easier than those about managing parents and staff. Through the process of answering the questions, he realizes that his work on the CLT is just the beginning. There are so many other facets of leadership he has to think about. However, Gavin also realizes that he does not have to go through these situations alone. He has Beth and Brad to help work out these situations, and now he has a functioning CLT to help him with other building-level goals.

Now that Gavin is beginning to move from surface to deep when it comes to his leadership, Michelle is starting to step back in how often she corresponds with him. They still have standing meetings every three weeks, and she is still available by email, phone, or Zoom, but Gavin is the principal and he needs to work through some of the usual trials and tribulations that all leaders face. Michelle and Gavin set a good foundation, and she wants to see how he makes decisions without always needing to rely on her. He even invites her to the next CLT meeting, saying that other teachers on the team have been asking if she would attend.

The decision making, and the trials and tribulations of leadership, will get a little more difficult for Gavin because the next CLT meeting will focus on addressing some difficult issues within the school community. Those issues, which all communities face, provide a good opportunity for leaders to build collective efficacy with staff. Gavin hopes that it will do the same at Naylor Middle School.

DISCUSSION QUESTIONS

Coaches and Leaders:

- How often would you communicate if you were coaching or being coached?
- Are there situations in your coaching relationships where you can apply the Goldilocks principle?

Leaders:

- How do you work in collaboration with the building-level union?
- What sort of leadership opportunities do you provide to your assistant principals?
- Do you have a building level team like the CLT?
  - If so, how often do you meet?
  - Are there co-chairs?
  - What is the focus of the CLT?

Coaches:

- How do you coach in a way that provides surface- to deep-level learning?
  - In what ways have you seen this learning transfer into the leadership of those being coached?

TAKE ACTION

- Fill out the Principals' Self-Efficacy questionnaire.
- Look for a goal within your answers.
- Send out a survey to staff focusing on something you really want to know.
- Be vulnerable with staff. Lead by example.

PRIORITY I– COLLECTIVE EFFICACY

Through my *Finding Common Ground* blog with *Education Week* I have been fortunate enough to connect with hundreds of thousands of readers. From time to time I would put out surveys at the end of blogs that focused on leadership or teaching, and the survey would ask a variety of questions regarding feedback, instructional leadership, teaching strategies, and other topics.

One of the most popular blog posts over the last few years focused on leadership coaching. Hence the catalyst for writing this book. At the end of one of the blog posts on leadership coaching I asked leaders to fill out a survey. Approximately 250 leaders filled it out and wrote down what their most important priorities were and why they needed coaching to help them successfully address those priorities. In this chapter, we begin with the first priority, and it focuses on collective efficacy.

My concern with collective efficacy is that the phenomenon is at risk of being like one of our favorite songs. At first, we love to hear it and play it over and over again. We listen for certain parts of the song, and we even start looking for songs by the same singer, band, or composer. Suddenly, we get tired of the song and hope it doesn't come on the radio when we are driving around town. Collective efficacy is very important, and we have to make sure we don't use the words too often and have our staff tune us out.

Many leaders want to know how to inspire collective efficacy and put it into practice, and in this chapter we watch Gavin and Michelle work all of that out.

Collective efficacy is a much more complicated concept than most people know. Michelle has helped Gavin understand collective efficacy over the months they have been working together. Gavin is working on it through the CLT process. Team members have established goals, and he has seen Beth and Brad, as well as other teachers, such as Cherise, Traesyn, and Brian, take more active roles in the group.

Although things are moving in the right direction, there are other areas for Gavin to think about, such as the following:

- How will he find a better balance between being reactive and proactive?
- How will he have more productive classroom observations when he has so many to do that he just wants to get them done?
- How will he authentically meet with Beth and Brad on a regular basis?
- How will he be sure that the PLCs in the building are taking a deep dive into learning rather than just compliantly meeting the seat time that the district dictates?
- How will he involve the community in stakeholder groups that he knows are necessary to move the building climate along?
- How will he gain the trust of the teachers and staff?

Welcome to the mind of a leader. The questions that come up in our mind, as well as those that come up in real life, often distract us from our focus, which affects our time management. Additionally, Michelle read an article in *The Wall Street Journal* by Daniel Pink (2018), which discussed how people go through cycles every day and how they can find their hidden rhythms. Pink said that we each have peak times, trough times, and rebound times in our day.

Michelle learned the following from the article (Pink, 2018):

The peak—During this part of the day, our executive functioning and concentration are at their best.

The trough—Our executive functioning plummets during the afternoon. A study in Denmark found that students who were randomly assigned to take tests in the afternoon performed at a level equivalent to having missed two weeks of school.

The rebound—For most people, this is the late afternoon and early evening. It's the best time to be creative.

Michelle understands this may have implications for leaders, particularly what time of day is most beneficial for different activities. As a general rule when it comes to time management, Michelle knows that understanding this cycle of peak times and trough times can really help those she coaches maximize their potential.

Additionally, Michelle understands that leaders think about the opportunity cost. If they are focusing on one thing, they understand that there is something else that is not getting their time and attention. Overall, leaders suffer from this opportunity cost when considering work/life balance. If leaders are the first to go into school every day and the last to leave, they may look really good to the central office because they are working hard, but at home the perspective may be very different. Spouses or partners at home are being left to their own devices and often feel like they are taking second place to the job of the leader. Gavin is experiencing this but he keeps telling himself that it will change after he gets a few more years under his belt.

Michelle understands that the importance of time management cannot be understated, but neither can the idea of understanding one's current reality, which is where she can have an enormous impact on Gavin's growth as a leader.

Additionally, this is where collective efficacy plays an important role for Gavin, because he has two assistant principals who count on him for guidance. He could be working in partnership with them more and more.

Unfortunately, Gavin still hasn't given them enough autonomy to make a decision without consulting him first. What this means for Gavin is that his time management is at risk because he has two assistant principals who have been enabled instead of empowered.

How Can Gavin Maximize His Time?

On Wednesday afternoon, Michelle arrives for their meeting to further talk through Gavin's goal. "How did the self-reflection activity work out for you?" Michelle asks. Although Gavin had his doubts about coaching, he realizes through the research on leadership self-efficacy and his trust issues in school that he needs to give coaching his all, or he is not going to be successful.

"I have to admit," Gavin begins slowly, "some of the questions were eye-opening. I actually poured a glass of wine before I answered because I needed to calm my nerves a bit and relax."

Michelle chuckles a bit.

"I realized I've been trying to go it alone, and the research even says that's not beneficial for a leader." After he finishes his sentence, he looked at Michelle with a pensive expression.

"Well, I think you just may have figured out why I'm here," Michelle answers with a smile.

Gavin and Michelle both discuss how some of his actions have led to enabling more than empowering. The assistant principals have to run every decision past him, and the teachers are handing in their lesson plan books on a rotation every six weeks, along with their notes from their department PLCs. Gavin admits that he doesn't always read the lesson plan books or the PLC notes, but he was requiring this because he was feeling insecure. "How did I become that guy?" he asks.

"That guy?" Michelle is a bit confused by what he was saying.

"You know, that kind of leader that feels the need to control everything because I'm insecure? I worked for a leader like that and swore I would never do it. And here I am," he says. His eyes water a bit. He is upset, confused, and feels stuck.

"Well, the important part is that you recognize it and want to change. Many leaders never recognize it," Michelle says, putting her hand on his shoulder.

"I feel like CLT is still an us versus them situation," Gavin admits. "I really need our group to focus on learning now that we have built some momentum, but I worry that my actions from before are hurting me now," he confides.

Michelle knew this would be difficult, and she hands Gavin a book on collaborative inquiry and collective efficacy by Jenni Donohoo (2017). In the book, Donohoo illustrates why it's difficult to build teacher voice, because the present feeling of voice is based on all of the previous experiences. Michelle shows Gavin a drawing of a ladder that Donohoo uses to illustrate the different types of teacher involvement in school decision making. Gavin sees that teachers' level of involvement can range from manipulation and decoration to teacher-initiated direct action and shared decision making.

Gavin studies the illustration. "Wow. That's quite the ladder," he says.

"Which step do you think highlights your stakeholder process?" Michelle asks.

Gavin takes some time to think about it. "I don't feel like I manipulate people to be a part of the process. And they do have a voice, so they've been a bit more than decoration or tokenism." Gavin pauses for a few seconds. "I have to admit that we have been pretty solidly number 4. My teachers are informed about and then assigned action," he says.

Michelle nods her head in agreement.

"Hey. Let yourself off the hook. You're trying to change these circumstances. Remember what we said about self-efficacy? It's situational, and this has been one group setting where you haven't felt efficacious. That's why we're working on it," she says.

Gavin wants the group to be less compliantly engaged and more authentically engaged. He realizes though, that Michelle is right. He's ready to move forward with collaboration, but the group isn't there yet based on their shared experiences with his so far, which means that they don't really believe they have a voice. Gavin needs to work on that with the group, and every conversation he has from now on will either build on that voice or detract from it.

Coach's Corner

Do What You Love

- Write down everything you are responsible for as a leader.
- Highlight the responsibilities that you most enjoy.
- How many of the items on the list focus on learning or building relationships? Most should.
- Spend as much of your time as possible working toward the highlighted activities.

Every leadership position comes with jobs we like to do and jobs we wish we didn't have to do. This exercise is meant to get leaders to highlight what they like to do and try to spend more time on those projects rather than the jobs they dislike.

Coach's Corner

Beware of Educational Jargon

Too often we use educational jargon like feedback, fidelity, and rigor. Although well-meaning and important parts of the learning process, those words are not always clearly defined in schools.

- Make sure that there is a common understanding of the words you use.

- After the words are clearly defined, make sure that those words aren't being used to force people into compliance. Make sure they are being used to empower learning.

  o Too often instructional coaches have been used as compliance officers. They go from room to room asking teachers why they aren't pacing at the right time or doing something with fidelity. It becomes top-down coaching as opposed to partnership coaching.

- In addition to defining the words, there need to be success criteria, which means that teachers and students need to understand what it looks like to successfully meet that criteria. For example, what does effective feedback actually look like?

Michelle reminds Gavin that there are four major categories of experience that influence self-efficacy (Bandura, 1977):

Personal performance accomplishments—A challenging activity brings out the strongest indicators for changing self-efficacy. When looking at leadership coaching, it's really important that the goal a leader and coach work on together is somewhat challenging. Have you ever put together furniture from IKEA? That's a challenging accomplishment and referred to as the IKEA effect.

Vicarious experiences—When we collaborate with others and witness the way they go about a challenging activity, we can learn through this vicarious experience. Some of our best ideas come from those colleagues we work with.

Social persuasion—Although this has negative connotations, it is deeply rooted in positive feedback. Positive feedback helps increase a person's level of self-efficacy. The coach helps build credibility in the coaching relationship by inspiring the leader to focus on a goal and then provides feedback to the leader about that goal.

Physiological condition—Last, and most important, social and emotional well-being matters because it contributes to a person's level of self-efficacy. It's one of the reasons why Stephen Covey (1990) told us to "sharpen the saw."

Michelle believes that effective coaching can play a part in each of these categories. By setting goals, working toward those goals, and receiving feedback from school stakeholders and the leadership coach, leaders have the opportunity to learn a great deal about themselves.

Taking into account the definition provided by the National College of Coaching and Leadership, Michelle, and leadership coaches like her, become very important in the acquisition of resources necessary for the learning taking place during the coaching cycle. In this coaching relationship, Gavin applies those methods learned through the dialogue he has with Michelle. Michelle understands that not only does she need to ensure that Gavin meets his goals, which will result in a positive impact on student learning, but she also must provide evidence of the impact she has had on him at the end of the coaching cycle. We should always understand our impact.

Coach's Corner

Strategies to Increase Trust in Schools

- Treat teachers like professionals.
- Greet them in the main office.
- Find something good about their teaching practices.
- Point out areas where they have a positive impact on the school community and/or students.
- Build their self-esteem by getting to know them through individual conversations.
- Don't send blanket emails when you should be having one-to-one conversations.

"We also have to remember that research shows that, as a principal, you are being asked to do more with less at times. In order to really maximize your leadership, you need to work collectively with Beth and Brad but also with the staff. Through that collective action, we build collective efficacy," Michelle explains to Gavin.

Gavin nods his head in agreement and says, "I feel like teachers are dealing with quite a bit these days. Our poverty rate has gone up from 15% to 35% over the last four years, and we have a lot of students who come to us suffering from trauma."

Michelle shakes her head, validating Gavin's feelings. "The reality is that there has been an increase in students who suffer from trauma, and one of the affects is that the adults in school can suffer from vicarious trauma," Michelle says. "We get so wrapped up in the lives of our students that we vicariously feel that trauma that they are experiencing. It is ever the more reason that we work collectively, because all of this has an effect on our school climate," she says.

Coaching Corner

Coaching Your Assistant Principals

As a leader, how do you coach your assistant principals? Too often, assistant principals are left to handle discipline and are given tasks the principal doesn't want to do. It's almost like a rite of passage in some of the districts I work in. How do you treat your assistant principals differently?

- Do you set goals with them?
- What kind of feedback do you give them?
- What evidence have you collected to show you are having an impact on the assistant principals you work with?

It's a difficult balance between focusing on the social–emotional needs of students and their academic needs as well. Michelle explains that through building collective efficacy with staff, leaders can work collectively to address the academic and social–emotional learning needs of students. Teachers cannot do this alone, which is why collective efficacy is so important. There are many ways to build collective efficacy. One option is to co-construct professional development options with teachers regarding issues happening in the building and use faculty meetings as the venue for professional development to address those issues. For example, if teachers and leaders are trying to address the issues that come with student trauma, they may use a faculty meeting to work with an outside agency, such as a mental health organization, to learn different ways to address the needs of those students who experience trauma.

Additionally, leaders and teachers may use collaborative inquiry (Donohoo & Velasco, 2016), which is a four-stage model where that helps build collective efficacy around a problem of practice. The four-stage model is as follows:

- Teams identify student learning needs.
- Teachers develop a question about a particular link between professional practice and student results.
- Teachers test new approaches in their classrooms while gathering evidence and artifacts.
- Teams collectively analyze data to assess the impact of their actions and determine their next steps (Donohoo & Velasco, 2016).

In the End

Leadership is about understanding self-efficacy and how to build collective efficacy and can lead to an enormous amount of growth on the part of a staff. We live in complicated times, and leaders cannot do it alone. Everyone feels efficacious in one area and a lack of efficacy in others. For example, a high school leader may not feel efficacious when it comes to teacher observations, and the following illustration tells the story of what can happen (see Figure 7.1).

To get the most out of the situations that matter, like teacher observations, we need to understand that we learn and grow through collective efforts. We, as leaders, need to acknowledge that we feel insecure around content we don't understand (i.e., chemistry, mechanical engineering, STEM, etc.) and should ask high-quality questions of those teachers

Figure 7.1   Why Self-Efficacy Matters

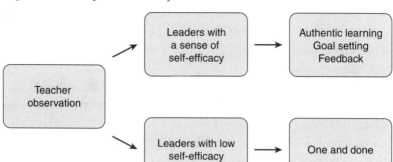

before the formal observation takes place. Only then can we decide together what the leader should look for, so that he or she can offer quality feedback to teachers.

In Gavin's case, he was vulnerable with the CLT because he was out of other options as far as bringing staff together and fostering trust. He knew that he was drowning in self-doubt and it was affecting his relationships with his assistant principals and staff. He began to trust the coaching process, and as he saw positive changes rather quickly, he kept going forward. He knows that he is not yet out of the woods when it comes to building trust with staff. And as we all know based on our leadership experiences, we sometimes take one step forward and two steps back.

Gavin's focus on establishing a CLT is really important, but it needs to be deeper. Too often schools have a building-level stakeholder group, but it doesn't accomplish much, and it doesn't focus on the root causes associated with low morale in the building. Group members look for Band-Aids, like having more celebrations, which are important but tend to be surface level. Those building-level groups do not look at their impact in the building. In order for a CLT to be effective, and to be more than just a group of adults who meet monthly, the team must a strong focus on student learning, and we can see that Gavin is moving in that direction.

In the next chapter, Gavin will explore one of the most intimidating dynamics of school leaders, and it's one that came up in my survey of leaders as a main priority. That priority is communication, and it ties directly into both teacher self-efficacy and leadership self-efficacy. Communication is totally dependent on the strength of belief of the teacher or leader.

Over the years, the use of social media by schools has risen, but there are still leaders and teachers who are nervous about what to post or tweet. Additionally, even though there are so many tools at our fingertips that we can use to communicate, communication is still an issue because too often we focus on one-sided monologue instead of dialogue. Effective communication is an area of need for leaders, because regardless of whether they talk face-to-face, over email, or on the phone, issues still arise.

DISCUSSION QUESTIONS

Coaches and Leaders:

- How can self-efficacy impact leaders?
- How do you feel about the progression of the CLT at Naylor Middle School?

Leaders:

- How many meetings within the school do you control?
- Looking at Donohoo's (2017) ladder of teacher involvement in shared decision making in school, where do you stand?
  - Where would teachers say they stand on Donohoo's (2017) ladder of teacher involvement in the shared decision-making process?

Coaches:

- How do you think Michelle should coach Gavin through the CLT process?
- What resources would you offer?

TAKE ACTION

Make a list of the ways you raise efficacy through the following experiences:

- Personal performance accomplishments
- Vicarious experiences
- Social persuasion
- Physiological condition

Reflect on how you spend your time as a leader. What do you do during your peak, trough, and rebound times?

- Do you maximize your peak time?
- What activity can you do during your trough time to get you up and moving?
- What do you find yourself doing during your rebound time?

8

PRIORITY II—
COMMUNICATION

J ust because communication is second on the list doesn't mean it's less important than collective efficacy. The reality is that leaders are judged on their communication all the time. Whether they communicate too much or not enough, one way or another they will hear about it.

Communication is an interesting topic, especially when we start considering how we communicate with families. Recently, I finished teaching a five-day competency-based learning class for the University of Oklahoma and the Oklahoma State Department of Education. It was a cohort program of 25 leaders who were either assistant principals or new principals.

On the last day of our time together I asked the whole group to stand up and shout out one of their favorite ways of communicating and engaging with families. As they shouted their responses, I realized it came down to three common themes:

- **Informational**—Information leaders believe families need to be kept informed (i.e., important dates, emergencies, etc.).

- **Relationship Building**—This is a time for leaders, teachers, and families to dialogue with one another (i.e., parent meetings, morning drop-off, PTA/PTO meetings, etc.).
- **Academic**—This includes events at school that focus on learning (i.e., game nights, math night, Science Fair, etc.).

This made me wonder which of these ways we communicate the most. When Gavin started his leadership experience, his most-used form of communication was providing information to families, which I refer to as one-sided communication. It's not that one-sided communication is bad, but it should not be the only form of communication we are known for as leaders.

It is my hope that with Michelle's help and guidance, Gavin will move into the dialogue type of communication. Perhaps as he builds collective efficacy among staff, teachers will assist him in providing more student learning information (i.e., what students are learning in schools) to families.

Michelle often arrives early for her meetings with Gavin. As their relationship has progressed, Gavin has begun to engage more and more. One time she arrived at their meeting early as usual and he told her he had a surprise for her. He walked her to a mostly empty room that had a desk.

"I know you like to arrive early so we had a space cleared for you. It's not much because space is a hot commodity around here," he said with a smile. "If we're going to work together all year, I'd like you to have a space if you want to come in early or hang out a bit late," he said.

Before she could thank him for the space he got a call on his walkie-talkie that there was a fight in the hallway between two students and he ran out. Michelle was pretty touched by the gesture and often arrived early and sat in the office to catch up on notes or review research on her laptop. Although Gavin didn't directly say much in the interaction, the act was a pretty big step in positive communication. It was a gesture communicating that he wanted her around, which was a bit different from their earlier meetings.

Coincidentally, Michelle has been thinking a lot about the leadership priority of communication. She knows people have numerous ways to communicate these days. Adults and students use social media tools like Twitter, Facebook, Instagram, Voxer, Snapchat, and others, but she isn't sure whether social media tools lead to deeper communication or are just a surface-level way of promoting the individual's way of thinking.

In her personal life, she has friends who unfriended each other based on the candidate they voted for in the presidential race or in other state and regional elections. She decided to take a break from Facebook due to conservative and liberal friends posting polarizing comments on their pages just to get "friends" to be on their side of the discussion. It was all too much, and Michelle understands that all of that "communication" bleeds into the school.

Adults and students have polarizing beliefs, which have an impact on their communication with each other. Adults blame students for being mean and bullying each other on social media, and then they go home and post negative comments and unfriend other people who don't agree with them. Michelle knows that effective communication is more than just a priority, because ineffective communication can destroy relationships.

Relationships are important. Everyone knows this, but it seems as though some principals and teachers forget it from time to time. Michelle has been reading Hattie's work on teacher–student relationships (e.g., Hattie, 2012a, 2012b), which indicates that the effect size is .72. Those relationships hold that effect size consistently even though other influences that Hattie researched got smaller. Influences like school leadership went from .39 in 2012 to .33 in 2017. However, the effect size for teacher–student relationships stayed the same.

Michelle knows that communication, which is one of the main priorities of leaders, is all about relationships. If leaders foster authentic relationships with as many staff, students, and families as possible, communication will be easier, even if it isn't always positive. Michelle has read and reread Stephen Covey's (1990) work and knows about his emotional bank account. He wrote and lectured that we all have an emotional bank account, there are times when we make deposits and other times when we make withdrawals. In Gavin's case, he had been making withdrawals, and Michelle was working with him to start making more deposits.

Additionally, Michelle has been reading Jenni Donohoo's (Donohoo, 2017; Donohoo & Velasco, 2016; see also Bryk & Schneider, 2003) work on collective efficacy, because Gavin's goal involving the CLT process was steeped in collective efficacy. He wanted to build it among the group, and hopefully that would create a grassroots effort to build collective efficacy among staff. In her collective efficacy work, Donohoo (2017) listed six enabling conditions that are necessary to raise efficacy:

- Advanced teacher influence
- Goal consensus
- Knowledge about each other's work
- Cohesive staff
- Responsiveness of leadership
- Effective systems of intervention

These conditions are essential to Gavin's ability to foster trusting relationships with staff and students. Every one of his CLT meetings is an opportunity to build collective trust among staff. All of this reminds Michelle of Bryk and Schneider's (2003) work on relational trust. Relational trust is central to Gavin's pursuit to build on Donohoo's (2017) enabling conditions.

ENABLING CONDITIONS

In a study of over 400 elementary schools in Chicago, Bryk and Schneider (2003) found that, "social trust among teachers, parents, and school leaders improves much of the routine work of schools and is a key resource for reform" (p. 40). Michelle understands that there are four important elements for relational trust in Bryk and Schneider's work:

Respect—"Social respect comes from the kinds of social discourse that take place across the school community. Respectful exchanges are marked by genuinely listening to what each person has to say and by taking these views into account in subsequent actions. Even when people disagree, individuals can still feel valued if others respect their opinions" (Bryk & Schneider, 2003, p. 42).

Personal regard—"Such regard springs from the willingness of participants to extend themselves beyond the formal requirements of a job definition or a union contract" (Bryk & Schneider, 2003, p. 42).

Competence in core responsibilities—"School community members also want their interactions with others to produce desired outcomes. For example, Teachers want supportive work conditions for their practice, which depends on the capacity of the school principal to fairly, effectively, and efficiently manage basic school operations" (Bryk & Schneider, 2003, p. 42).

Personal integrity—"Integrity also demands that a moral-ethical perspective guides one's work. Although conflicts frequently arise among competing individual interests within a school community, a commitment to the education and welfare of children must remain the primary concern" (Bryk & Schneider, 2003, p. 42).

As she waits in the office for Gavin so they can have a little conference time before heading around to do some walk-throughs, Michelle pulls out her notes to look at Donohoo's (2017) list. Michelle knows that Gavin is starting to advance teacher influence through the CLT process, and through that work they are also coming to consensus about goals. However, Michelle also knows that Gavin has more work to do in this area individually with teachers before they complete authentic walk-throughs and the formal teacher observation process, all of which need to focus on learning.

When it comes to knowledge about each other's work, Michelle knows that Gavin is emerging in this area. He is beginning to flip faculty meetings around a common learning goal so teachers can share best practices. CLT members brainstormed ideas like feedback, authentic PLC conversations, and the walk-through process. However, Michelle definitely wants Gavin to begin thinking about fostering a school climate where teachers can step into each other's classrooms as well, and that all goes back to Bryk and Schneider's (2003) work on relational trust.

Over the months they have been working together, Michelle observes several areas of strength in Gavin's leadership in regard to Donohoo's (2017) enabling conditions, particularly his desire to have a cohesive staff, be responsive to staff concerns, and create effective systems of intervention. Gavin set up some stakeholder groups, and they were becoming more effective, mostly because he was actually listening and asking questions instead of solely providing information. Other times, Gavin would send out emails that resulted in Anika and Janelle meeting with him in a union capacity because most of the building was up in arms over what he said in the email. This varied from changes in the schedule due to a lack of substitutes in the morning to extra help with lunch duty. Gavin often found that when Anika and Janelle said the whole building was up in arms, it was actually just a loud minority of teachers. It was something Gavin addressed every time he asked Anika and Janelle for the actual numbers of teachers who complained. Gavin is learning not to over-react to these types of situations and soon realizes that some of the people who have been objecting to his communications are simply misunderstanding them. Michelle is confident that Gavin will grow through these issues and learn to create more opportunities for positive communication.

Coach's Corner

Assess Your Communication Practices

Do you differentiate your communication?

- Do you talk to the loud minority face-to-face before you send an email?
- Do you talk with groups about the topic before you send an email further explaining the issue?
- Do you soften your approach in person with some staff members and become more blunt with other staff members?

COACHING COMMUNICATION

In their relationship, Michelle and Gavin have found several ways to communicate. Michelle often refers to the Goldilocks principle because she doesn't want to communicate so much that she enables Gavin, but she also doesn't want to communicate so little that they don't have a chance to establish and foster a relationship where Gavin can get over his insecurities of having a coach. Besides the biweekly visits in person, where Michelle spends a few hours to a full day depending on their goal for each day, Michelle and Gavin communicate via Voxer. Having the walkie-talkie app on their phones is a great way to overcome the obstacles of catching each other by phone. Gavin has all of his duties as a principal, and Michelle has other leaders she is coaching, so Voxer gives them both the flexibility they need to dive deeper into conversations.

Coach's Corner

Establish Communication Frequency

Communication between coaches and leaders, or leaders who want to coach assistant principals, can be a challenge. What is too much? What is too little? Here are some items to consider:

- If we live close to those we coach, we have an opportunity to visit often. If we are coaching assistant principals, we see them numerous times each day.
- Regardless of proximity, set up a schedule of when meetings will happen. At first, especially when establishing a relationship with those we coach, we need to communicate often.
- We should always be working to empower and not enable.

Additionally, Michelle and Gavin decided to hold Zoom meetings from time to time because it gave them a chance to talk face-to-face virtually. Those meetings were usually 30 minutes or less, enough time for them to check in with each other. Michelle's responsiveness to Gavin's needs definitely

helped him become more comfortable with the coaching relationship. Through their interactions virtually and in reality,
Gavin learned a great deal about communication, so much so
that he began to use some of the same communication techniques with his assistant principals and teachers. It was not
always perfect. Much like what other leaders experience, communication is a case of one step forward and two steps back.

Gavin's Changing Communication

- Gavin has stopped multitasking. When someone comes to talk with
  him, he puts his phone down or steps away from the computer.
- He spends more time in the hallways. He purchased a stand-up desk
  and rolls it into the hallway so he can spend more time talking with
  students.
- Before meetings with his assistant principals, he writes down three
  questions he wants to ask them, and he makes a conscious effort not
  to dominate the conversation. It is all about dialogue, not one-sided
  monologue.

COMPLICATIONS OF COMMUNICATION

When it comes to communication, we all suffer from the same
fate from time to time. Michelle knows that we often read
emails with the tone we are feeling and not necessarily the
tone for which it is meant. When she was a principal, Michelle
found herself answering emails too curtly on the days that she
felt the most frustrated, and on the other days, when she felt
rested and had time for reflection, she answered the emails
with a great deal more thought.

Michelle knows that it's hard being a leader. Everyone
wants a piece of your time, and it doesn't matter whether
you are on your way to a crisis or just going to the bathroom,
someone stops you because they need something. There are
so many ways for teachers, students, and families to get the

attention of a leader like Gavin. Email is one such form of communication, which makes it easier for parents or staff to get in touch with a leader, but email has been a double-edged sword since it was introduced to schools in the late 1990s. What became a new and easy way to communicate also created new issues.

Leaders like Michelle understand that it's not just the method of communication that is important but also the topic that is being communicated. Leaders find their biggest issues when they are trying to communicate about initiatives or difficult situations, like personnel matters, disagreements between students, or controversial topics like transgender bathrooms. Leaders are involved in thousands of conversations a day, and those conversations don't always go well. Michelle knows that in order to combat those negative interactions, leaders must be proactive and take the time to build relationships with each stakeholder in a school, one conversation at a time. She thinks of it as a grassroots effort to build a positive climate and culture. For Gavin, he needs to start with his assistant principals.

Stuck in the Middle . . . Again

It's hard being a building principal, because we often feel stuck in the middle of district initiatives and teacher needs. Is there a way we can get ourselves out of the middle?

- What is the district initiative?
- How was it communicated to teachers?
- When stepping back to process the initiative, is it ultimately going to benefit the students?
- Is it possible for the principal to find one blog or article explaining the initiative and send it to staff a few days before the faculty meeting so they can obtain some surface-level knowledge? Use the faculty meeting to go deeper into what the initiative is all about.

The reality is that principals are in the middle. Embrace it, and try to figure out a way to build a bridge between the district office and what teachers need.

COMMUNICATION WITH ASSISTANT PRINCIPALS

Michelle understands that Gavin's interactions with Beth and Brad should mirror the interactions Michelle has with Gavin. The luxury of having assistant principals is that it provides a think tank for the administrative team. Gavin now understands that he needs to approach his assistant principals as if he is a coach, because part of their experience of working together should empower Beth and Brad so they can move on to lead other buildings. If Beth and Brad are to be high-quality leaders, it begins with the team they build with Gavin and what they learn from that experience. If Gavin micromanages Beth and Brad, they are at risk of leading their own buildings in the same way, which could ruin the culture. If Gavin works on being more collaborative, Beth and Brad can learn through the experience and model collaborative leadership in their own buildings. Luckily, Gavin prefers to be more collaborative.

Gavin has grown in his leadership with his assistant principals. They have their own grade levels that they are responsible for, and they have stepped up to the plate during faculty meetings and the CLT process. They have even taken on the responsibility of engaging staff in more authentic PLCs that focus on learning as opposed to seat time where teachers do not accomplish much. Over that time, teachers have begun to see that they have a voice in the school climate and culture, so they take their meeting times more seriously, because they get to focus on goals they care about, as opposed to goals that are directed from their district.

COMMUNICATION WITH STAFF

Although communication is a priority for leaders, it also can be an obstacle. Leaders are at risk of being criticized for miscommunicating or communicating too little or not at all. However, in these days of using social media, branding our schools, and trying to get out effective messaging, Michelle understands that leaders like Gavin are at risk of overcommunicating as much as they are at risk of communicating too little.

Communication is supposed to be a two-way street in schools. Faculty meetings, emails, and one-to-one conversations happen numerous times a day, and most of the time the communication that takes place between a teacher and leader is remembered by the teacher for a long time. Gavin once made the comment to Michelle that he was surprised how many teachers could recite something he had said a year prior during his first year as principal. At first he said it seemed like a joke, but then he realized that the reality is that teachers and staff remember the conversations they have with their leader. That is why communication is so important.

Michelle knows that if leaders like Gavin are going to work more collaboratively with their whole school community, they need to understand the complexities of helping adults, because leadership is about working with and helping others. Michelle has long been a fan of instructional coaching expert Jim Knight's work and always returns to his list of five areas that make it complicated for coaches to help adults: change, identity, thinking, status, and motivation (Knight, 2011). Michelle believes it is time to review this list again.

Change—Educators are asked to change all the time. Why change? Is it because there is a new leader in town? If a leader is looking to make changes to something in school that potentially affects the community, how is the leader communicating that change?

Identity—From a community perspective, schools have an identity. How does a leader's communication fit in with the identity of the school community?

Thinking—If leaders do the thinking for their community without community involvement, there is potential for major resistance. How has the community been involved in the thinking, and how will this be communicated to those who are not present?

Status—Leaders need to understand that the status they carry with them in the position is the reason why people seek them out for a variety of reasons. Leaders need to accept their status and move on carefully because it plays a part in the communication they have with all stakeholders.

Motivation—Do leaders communicate in a way that will motivate stakeholders? Or do they communicate in a way that puts stakeholders in the position of being compliant listeners?

Michelle sees too many leaders who do the thinking for their staff and then get upset with those same staff members when they seem enabled rather than engaged in stakeholder groups. Rhetoric around teaching has not been kind. Too often the national rhetoric has been that teachers are not doing enough for students or that our system is failing. Michelle understands all too well that this negative rhetoric has resulted in less people going into the teaching profession, and more teachers are looking to be told what to do because they feel they have no voice, and all of this makes communication very complicated but highly important.

Coach's Corner

Communication Mistakes to Avoid

There are some simple mistakes we make when it comes to communication:

- Dominating the conversation. Too often we talk without asking questions. As Stephen Covey (1990) said, we should listen to understand instead of to reply.
- Entering into a conversation with a rigid agenda or with the answer we already want. Don't have the conversation if you enter into it with the same answer you want to walk away with.

What can we do? Video record ourselves in a conversation or at a faculty meeting. Do we talk with people or at them?

To help raise the level of teacher voice, we have to enter into our conversations with those adults who work in school as if what they have to say is just as important as what we have to say. When it comes to teacher voice in schools, Michelle often reviews the work of Russ Quaglia and Lisa

Lande. In a survey of over 8,000 staff members, Quaglia and Lande (2014) found the following (see Figure 8.1).

Ruben and Gigliotti (2016) found that there are three types of communication practices on the part of leaders—classic linear, interactional, and systems—all of which are defined here.

Classic Linear—This view suggests that if a leader intends to accomplish a particular goal or communicate a specific message, he or she creates and transmits the message and the process seemingly plays out in a very linear and predictable manner.

Interactional—An interactional perspective attempts to capture more of the complexity and two-way influence between a leader and a follower. The interactional perspective recognizes that communication is not a one-way process.

Systems—This view of communication focuses directly on the way people create, convey, select, and interpret the messages that inform and shape their lives. The authors go on

Figure 8.1   Stakeholder Engagement in School

Curiosity and Creativity Statements	Percentage in Agreement
At school 1 am encouraged to be creative.	69%
Building administration is open to new ideas.	67%
1 enjoy learning new things.	99%
School inspires me to learn.	83%
Our school is a dynamic and creative learning environment.	67%
Staff work in a collaborative manner.	72%
Meaningful professional development opportunities exist in my district.	54%
1 feel comfortable asking questions in staff meetings.	68%

to suggest that this perspective recognizes that some of these messages are intentionally created; others are produced accidentally. Some messages are constructed to achieve specific influence goals or intentions; others may be unconsciously created by their initiator with no specific purpose in mind.

Gavin's experience has always been the classic linear method, and that's what teachers have been used to. During CLT meetings, he makes a conscious effort to be very open and honest and states that the CLT is not about him but about the collective thoughts of the group. The more he models that in the CLT, his faculty meetings, and his daily conversations, the more staff begin to open up, which will help get to the heart of the issues.

If communication is to be a priority for leaders, coaches can help leaders understand the complexities of communication. It is not merely about sending an email or having a conversation. Within seconds of initiating some sort of communication, leaders need to understand what the purpose is, how the audience might receive that communication, whether the audience wants that communication, and whether they are willing to receive feedback after the communication. Leaders also need to be aware of what the audience might do with that feedback after they communicate.

Coach's Corner

Feedback Triggers to Watch Out For

In the best-selling book, *Thanks for the Feedback: The Science and Art of Receiving Feedback Well*, Douglas Stone and Sheila Heen (2015) found that we all experience feedback triggers when receiving feedback:

- Truth Triggers—We think the feedback is untrue or unhelpful.
- Relationship Triggers—We don't believe the person giving us feedback has the credibility to do so.
- Identity Triggers—The feedback we receive shatters the identity we created for ourselves.

All of this plays an important role in how leaders communicate, and coaches can work with leaders on their communication skills by prereading communication that goes out, having dialogue around the purpose of the communication, and even role-playing with the leader to foster growth in the area of one-to-one communication.

Coaching Challenging Conversations

Michelle can tell that Gavin feels a bit relieved that the CLT process continues to go well after some initial bumps and bruises. He thanks her for talking through the process with him over the phone because it boosted his confidence as he entered into the first meeting. He even remarked that several of the members came to him afterward to say they were excited to be on the committee. However, he also knows that some are still cautious, but that is OK. He actually looks at that as a good challenge to keep him on his toes as he goes through the year with the CLT.

Gavin explains to Michelle that during a few of the meetings, he was challenged by the co-chairs, which led to deeper learning on his part. In other meetings, he felt comfortable to challenge the co-chairs or Beth and Brad. What he found is that he is modeling to others how to challenge each other's thinking without being destructive. Not everyone on the CLT feels comfortable doing this, but more of the members have begun to dive into the process of challenging other members of the team.

Coach's Corner

Ways to Challenge in Conversations

Some of the best ways to challenge is by asking questions. Here are a few examples:

- I wonder . . . what led you to believe that? I wonder . . . what led you to that conclusion?
- What evidence do you have to support that?

Michelle is happy to hear about the progress, and thanks Gavin for all of his hard work. Michelle knows that social persuasion is one of the biggest contributors to self-efficacy, and positive feedback is a major aspect of social persuasion. Gavin has been working hard, and Michelle wants to make sure that she thanks him for his effort.

Gavin continues to talk about the CLT meeting that focused on student learning.

"What are you hoping to get out of the process," Michelle asks. It is a good question and one they discussed quite a bit in their CLT meeting the day before.

"We've had a sense that we come in every day and do the same thing and that the same students are engaged and the same ones are not. We're trying something new. We're hoping that by the end of the year we can come up with some learner dispositions that all students can learn after we are done with this process," Gavin says.

"What dispositions are you thinking of using," Michelle asks.

"We've been throwing around the idea of using self-regulation, resiliency, and a few others, but we still have some work to do," Gavin responds. "We know that this year has been a growth year for us when it comes to the CLT process and building trust. Every representative on the CLT goes back to their constituency to discuss what we have been doing, and then we take some time to focus our professional learning and development around those efforts at our faculty meetings. We want student learning to be at the heart of our discussion. However, I know that focusing on learner dispositions this year would put all of that work at risk, so we are just trying to blend our learning in the CLT with student learning progressions and our faculty meeting learning around the same topic. Next year we can focus our efforts on what those dispositions will be. We have worked on the difference between authentic engagement and compliant engagement. We kind of worry that too many of our students are compliantly engaged. We want more than that," Gavin says, almost as if he can't believe everything they have covered, because he knows that it was hard work to get there.

Gavin pauses and then says, "We are also going to explore more in the area of social–emotional learning. We have talked a lot about how students need an emotional connection to school, but we still need to do a lot of work regarding inclusive education, which will be the next topic we discuss at the CLT."

"That is definitely a worthy and heavy goal," Michelle agrees.

In the End

One of the most important priorities for leaders is communication, but we know that communication is complicated. Recently, I was participating in a Voxer group, discussing my book on school climate, and the topic of communication came up. The school leaders taking part in the group gave specific examples of how some of their teachers created issues with families, and it didn't matter whether we were talking about face-to-face, email, or phone communication. We have numerous ways to communicate, and some people still stink at it.

There are simply times that leadership communication will not go well, and that is why building trust is so vitally important. Leaders need not look any further than the important work of Stephen Covey and the emotional bank account. There will be times when we make deposits and other times when we make withdrawals.

However, we can save ourselves a lot of pain and heartbreak if we take the time to walk away from a negative email and figure out how best to respond after we have had time to cool down. We shouldn't respond in haste, and more times than not, we should pick up the phone to call the sender of the email rather than repeating their same pattern of returning negativity with negativity.

In our continuing story with Gavin and Michelle, we have learned that his CLT process has had bumps and bruises along the way, which is also seen as an implementation dip. However, through modeling and moving forward, Gavin has been able to convince more and more stakeholders on the CLT that they have a voice.

Teacher voice is a really important topic. Too much rhetoric about education has not been kind, and teachers are suffering under the weight of that rhetoric. Leaders need to make sure that they send a countermessage to teachers that their voices matter. If teachers do not feel as though they have a voice in their schools, how will students ever believe they have a voice in their schools?

DISCUSSION QUESTIONS

Coaches and Leaders:

- How often as coaches and leaders do you communicate with each other?
  - In a best-case scenario, how often do you believe coaches and leaders should communicate?
- What are the forms of communication you most frequently use?

Leaders:

- How do you communicate with staff?
  - What have you learned about communication through a bad experience?
- How often do you meet with assistant principals?
  - Is the process seen as coaching or just going through important agenda items?
- In your stakeholder group, who runs the meetings?
  - Have you defined roles and expectations?

Coaches:

- Have you ever had communication with a leader you are coaching go wrong?

  ○ What did you do to resolve the issue?

- Has proximity played a part in how effective a coaching experience has been?

TAKE ACTION

- Make a list of the ways you communicate with families, staff, and students. Write down whether those forms of communication are informational, relationship building, or academic?

PRIORITY III—STUDENT AND COMMUNITY ENGAGEMENT

We know from the last chapter that there are leaders who focus on three ways to engage families, which are information, relationship building, and academic. How we communicate with students, families, and the larger community is important. Not for nothing, but I sometimes feel like education is under constant attack. We are accused of making too much money, working too little, or not achieving enough.

The other night I was having dinner with some coaches that I worked with at the University of Oklahoma through the Collaborative Leadership cohort, and we began discussing a Facebook page where families spoke negatively about their school. I typically refer to that as ripping on the school.

We commiserated about how we have all dealt with that before when we were education leaders, but then the conversation changed, because I said we need to own some of that. Negative posting about school for me came when we consolidated buildings and closed a school that had one classroom per grade level and absorbed the whole population. But the reality is that we still had to own some of the negativity.

When we explore this chapter with Gavin and Michelle, I want you to reflect on how you communicate with different stakeholders. Now, this is where John Hattie would chastise me a bit because he has a theory on reflection. He says that if we reflect on something without evidence, we are merely remembering it the way we think it happened, as opposed to the way it actually happened. So, if you're going to reflect, bring some evidence.

Now that the CLT process is moving in the right direction, Gavin wants to approach the group about focusing on a few issues that he thinks is worth their time. He believes the work they will do to address the issues will strengthen the level of collective efficacy among the CLT. Those issues are family engagement and community engagement, with a focus on student learning and engagement.

School leaders and teachers have long tried to find ways to involve families in their child's education, but Gavin attended a professional development session a while ago and the presenter talked about how schools tend to believe that family engagement should focus on how the school can deliver its message, as opposed to true dialogue between families and the school. Community engagement is something different. It goes beyond just the typical parental or family involvement conversation. In one of their previous meetings, Michelle explained to Gavin that in these days of social–emotional well-being and creating an inclusive environment to help engage minoritized students, community engagement means that sometimes schools have to work with outside organizations that have expertise that schools do not to maximize the potential of all learners, not just the ones who already fit in. Beth would be involved in this because it is the goal she established with Gavin.

Due to scheduling issues, Michelle could not attend their last CLT meeting, but she is able to make this one. Gavin begins the meeting by saying, "We have done a great deal of work together over the last few months, and I feel like we

have really come together as a group." Most of the stakeholders nod in agreement as Gavin continues to talk. Michelle
looks around the room to take in the body language.

"I feel like there are two issues that we could focus on
together, but they're not always going to be easy," Gavin says.
This statement definitely gets the attention of those sitting
around the table. "I really worry about the negative rhetoric
around schools, and it's hard for us to hear when we watch
the evening news or look at Facebook and Twitter. I know this
has come up in some our conversations as a group and in our
individual conversations with each other. I'm proud of what
we do here at Naylor, and I want our families to know because
if we are hearing negative messages at the state and national
level, then they are as well." There is a pause around the table.

Collaborative Leadership Team Explores Family Engagement

Janelle speaks up: "Gavin, I understand, but how do we do
more than we already are?"

Gavin can tell this is something others around the table are
wondering as well. "I have been working with my coach, and
I don't think it's about flooding more communication down
the pipeline to families, but I think we need to change the way
we do it," he says.

"How do we do that?" Janelle asks, with her arms folded.

//

Janelle's Story

Janelle has been a seventh- and eighth-grade ELA teacher
at Naylor Middle School for 30 years. To say she is an
institution within the institution is an understatement.
She has never even changed rooms in her 30-year tenure.
She is known for being fairly abrupt with students over
those years, but she doesn't consider that a problem.
Janelle believes that students need a tough teacher who

will hold them accountable. She thinks students of this age are becoming soft because they are too coddled by their parents.

Janelle has seen her share of principals come and go. Alan, her previous principal, left her alone, and she appreciated that. She typically saw him in her classroom when there was a discipline issue she needed help with or when she had to be observed twice every year. Besides that, they saw each other in the hallway and at the faculty meetings, and that was fine with her. Janelle felt that Alan lacked credibility in her content area and there wasn't much he could help her with when it came to teaching.

Besides having two master's degrees, one in literacy and the other in classical literature, Janelle has an administrative degree she has never formally used. Truthfully, she doesn't want to go to the "dark side" like so many of her colleagues. She believes she is better served working with students.

With this new administrative team, Janelle finds herself worried. Gavin talks a lot about collaboration, and Beth and Brad seem nice, but she is a bit tired of hearing about principals who want to collaborate. Janelle has always believed that teachers have their roles, which is with students, and leaders have their roles, which means patrolling the hallway and dealing with discipline.

However, she is beginning to like the fact that Gavin meets with her and Anika for their union meetings on Friday mornings. Alan never did that, and it shows that Gavin is open to listening to concerns. She enters those meetings with an open mind, but she always reminds herself that Gavin is an administrator. She wants to make sure the meetings don't become a place for him to share his propaganda.

As for the CLT, Janelle assumed Gavin created the group to impress his new coach and Dr. Coppola, the school superintendent. Janelle had run-ins with Dr. Coppola. Additionally, she heard from union leadership that Dr. Coppola wasn't always open to talking about issues, and there were some ongoing battles with high school teachers.

Janelle didn't mind being asked to be a part of CLT, because she secretly likes the status that comes along with being on a building-level team. It also gives her the opportunity to keep a watchful eye on the process that the stakeholders go through. She is concerned about some of the other people who volunteered because she thinks they are too quiet and can be pushed around by administration.

Janelle decides to have side conversations with a few of the teachers on the CLT after the first meeting to suggest that she may be the best fit for a co-chair position. She and Anika work well together, and the union has a vested interest in how the CLT functions. Janelle has been through too many collaborative processes that were not collaborative at all because the administrators already knew what they wanted before the meetings ever took place, and she wasn't going to allow the same thing to happen this time.

//

"Well, I'm not really sure," Gavin answers honestly. "I'm hoping we can figure that out together here."

Cherise, one of the quieter teachers on the team, begins ever so politely, "It seems like you might think, and I could be wrong, that you feel there is a problem with our family communication." She sits back, hoping she didn't say too much.

Truthfully, Gavin is really happy that Cherise spoke up. She has been finding her voice lately on the CLT, and that is a good thing. "I do. I feel like we talk at parents and not with them. I feel like we try to convey our message, but we don't always like it when families try to convey theirs," he says.

"But aren't we supposed to convey our message?" Janelle asks, a bit defensively.

"It's not that I don't think we should convey our message because we need times to communicate information. However, I feel like I want there to be more dialogue, and I think we have to discuss what we want out of our relationship with families," Gavin says, looking around the table. "I know it's not something we will solve today, but I'd like us to brainstorm some ideas."

Anika, who recently had a difficult parent meeting in which Gavin had to intervene, says, "I think Gavin's right. I just had a really awful meeting with a parent, and thankfully, it worked out at the end. But one of the things that came up is the way school communicates."

Janelle interrupts, "Parents always complain about the way school communicates. That's a complaint every year."

Anika responds, "Exactly. Isn't now the time we do something about it?"

Gavin is a bit shocked by how the conversation is going and realizes it is the first time members of the team are a bit raw and honest with one another. They spend another 20 minutes discussing communication issues.

Coach's Corner

Encourage Coachees to Assess Family Focus

School leaders should be asking the following:

- Do parents understand the language of learning? If not, how can we help them?
- Do we use too many educational words that families do not understand? Those words will become a wall instead of a bridge for families and schools.
- Do we have learner dispositions (i.e., resilience, persistence, self-awareness, etc.) for our school and do families know them?
- How do we seek feedback from our families? Do we change anything about our school community based on the feedback from those surveys?
- Do we ask families what we can do to help them?
- What resources do we offer our families in need?

First and foremost, their discussion focused on the fact that not all children live with their parents. Instead of looking at engagement as parental only, they need to expand their view and define it more as family engagement. Families look different, and if the school climate at Naylor Middle School was going to provide ways to make all families feel welcome and supported, the language needs to change first. Family engagement should be used because it encompasses the different types of families that are present in a school community. Understanding that, and using language to support it, will go a long way to begin building community engagement.

//

Anika's Story

Anika Arya has been a self-contained special education teacher for 35 years. She is shorter than most but stands tall against anyone who confronts her because she is not one to take a lot of grief from people. There are times when Anika stands up against administration and other times when she stands up against her colleagues. For Anika, it is not about loyalty to her colleagues or the union; she believes her job is to be loyal to her students, regardless of who she may have to fight with in the building.

What makes her stand out more than most is that she will help teachers de-escalate situations with students who are not even hers. There were times when Alan was dealing with students who were fighting with him, and Anika stepped in and got the students to calm down so that they could all get to the heart of the issues.

Due to her ability to de-escalate tense and volatile situations with students, and some adults, Anika was always one of the first people Alan called when he had to leave the building for a meeting, because he knew that people trusted her and would go to her if there was an issue. Alan seemed to trust Anika more than he trusted his assistant principals, and everyone including the assistant principals knew it. Some of that is due to the fact that they taught together for many years before Alan became a principal, but it was also because Alan felt that Anika was more competent than his assistant principals.

As for her counterpart on the CLT, Anika doesn't always like that Janelle approaches situations from a cynical viewpoint. Although Anika has been in her share of stakeholder groups that were not authentic when it came to offering teachers a voice in the process, she approaches each new stakeholder group as if it could be more authentic and inclusive. She likes Gavin because he seems to want teacher voice in the CLT, which is why she was happy to volunteer for the group and to be one of the co-chairs. Their Friday morning union meetings go well, and many times they don't even talk about issues in the building as much as they talk about compliance and accountability requirements coming from the state or federal level. She likes that the Friday morning meetings are usually about dialogue.

Secretly, Anika feels that she is getting soft at her age, because she has high hopes that Gavin is going to be a different kind of leader, especially after going through the coaching process with Michelle. She loves that he sent the staff such a thoughtful email explaining the CLT process and that he was so open about being coached by Michelle. Anika has seen principals who wanted to work with staff ultimately turn into administrators who wanted to control every situation. Although Gavin was a bit insecure in the first month of school after the students arrived, Anika notices that he is becoming more and more collaborative.

In the long run, Anika knows she is two years from retirement, and she really wants to help Naylor Middle School become a place where teachers and leaders work together for the benefit of the students. She strongly believes that Gavin is the one to do this.

The Collaborative Leadership
Team Realizes All Doesn't Mean All

Cherise speaks up again: "You said there were two issues you wanted us to discuss. Is the other one the minoritized population issue that Beth talked about at the last faculty meeting?"

Internally, Gavin is happy that Cherise is sitting up, leaning in, and taking an active role in the discussion, and Michelle had heard Cherise was quieter, so this is a win for Gavin, in Michelle's point of view. Gavin is going to make sure to say something to Cherise about it after the meeting. He plans to offer appreciative feedback because she needs to know how much Gavin appreciates the fact that she is working hard to step outside of her comfort zone and speak up.

As much as she is an outstanding teacher, Gavin noticed that she didn't always speak up in meetings, and yet he knew she had important insight for the group. She was a teacher leader, but she didn't know it yet, and now her leadership is beginning to come out in their conversations.

Gavin begins by saying, "The next one might be a little controversial, but I'm taking part in a Voxer group with a bunch of leaders I met through Twitter, and one of them began asking questions about how we all work with our minoritized groups. This has been a passion area for Beth, as we know, and I think we need to explore it further if we really want to engage all learners."

Beth had provided Gavin with the definition of minoritized students a few weeks earlier, and Gavin sent it out to staff before their last flipped faculty meeting, because he was noticing some changing trends in school, especially when the walk-through team looked at who was really engaged in each class. Harper (2012) explained the use of the word *minoritized* instead of *minority*:

Persons are not born into a minority status nor are they minoritized in every social context (e.g., their families, racially homogeneous friendship groups, or places of

worship). Instead, they are rendered minorities in particular situations and institutional environments that
sustain an overrepresentation of Whiteness. (p. 9)

All of the stakeholders knew this was going to be a topic
they would have to discuss, so Cherise isn't totally surprised
after Gavin explains the second of the two issues: "Like Beth
said at the faculty meeting, we have been having issues with
student engagement and discipline. As we went through the
evidence, we noticed a common theme. Many of the students
who are sent out of class are those students who would be
considered minoritized."

Beth comes from a counseling background, and minoritized populations was the topic for her master's thesis. She
also knows that this will be a very difficult topic for teachers
to face, discuss, and do something about together.

Brian Bellagio, a seventh- and eighth-grade social studies teacher who has a variety of arm tattoos and is popular
with his students, chimes in: "I've been thinking about this
one a lot. As you know I have had debates in class that work
out fairly well, but I could go deeper. However, I also have
concerns."

"What are your concerns?" Gavin asks, leaning into the
conversation.

Brian responds, "I know that we have seen an increase in
the number of transgender students in our school, which is
definitely a minoritized population, but we haven't done a
good job of figuring out how to include them. I feel like it's the
elephant in the room. Honestly though, I just worry because
this could be an explosive topic with families, and some of
our colleagues have spoken to me privately to say they have
no idea how to talk with these students, and they're worried
about administrative support. They're worried."

Gavin looks around the table and asks for other thoughts.
It is an interesting conversation because a few members
of the team are completely uncomfortable. Gavin can tell
because they don't speak and their body language is very
closed off. Others talk about how they had a nephew or niece

going through transition, and others are somewhere in the middle.

WORKING WITH OUTSIDE ORGANIZATIONS

They have a deep discussion about how they can include all minoritized populations, and Beth offers the idea of working with some outside community action groups that can help them address the issue of including minoritized populations. The outside group would work with teachers first, and the CLT would discuss how to move forward with those same groups in working with students. Due to the fact that Gavin addressed the minoritized student issue with staff at the last faculty meeting, they decide it is a good time to see if the community group can attend the last faculty meeting of the year. It isn't perfect timing, but it would force teachers to leave with something to reflect on for the following year.

Team members agree that they need to set some ground rules with the outside organization, because some of them had heard stories about how an outside group came in to work with staff in other schools but never took the time to understand the context of the schools or the student population, and the professional development sessions ended up missing the mark, which means opportunities were lost.

Coach's Corner

Encourage Community Engagement

It's important to work with outside organizations when trying to create an inclusive school climate. For example, if leaders are trying to find ways to create an environment safe for LGBTQ students (a minoritized population), they may need to work with an outside LGBTQ community center. However, leaders should keep the following in mind:

- Make sure that teachers working with the organization have vetted the resources. Sometimes outside organizations use overwhelmingly

(Continued)

(Continued)

large resources that can provide so much information that it becomes more about pushing an agenda than educating about the needs of the population.

- When working with outside organizations, make sure they understand the context in which teachers are working. Too often we use our own acronyms in our professions, and the organizations need to make sure they are using friendly language that students and teachers can easily understand.
- When working through controversial topics with an outside organization, make sure families are aware that this is happening. One way or another they will find out, and if leaders are reactive instead of proactive with the information, they make create even more work for themselves.

Additionally, outside of topics that are considered by many to be controversial, Gavin was becoming more aware that he needed to look at the whole community. In some school communities, the school is the only game in town. In many rural communities, the school is sometimes the only place where children can play outside of their homes. There are no malls, YMCAs, or recreation centers.

WHAT SHOULD COMMUNITY ENGAGEMENT LOOK LIKE?

Michelle and Gavin had discussed with Beth and Brad during an administration coaching meeting that, in daily conversations, education is a topic that often comes up because the way students act at their afterschool jobs has a direct impact on the conversations around school. Are students prepared for the workplace? When students work at the grocery stores, retail outlets, and other businesses that make up a community, are they showing their employers that they are prepared? For example, if a student worker cannot make change without looking at the register, or if he or she can't determine how to help or find the answer when a customer asks a question, what is the first thing that customer will think? What are leaders and teachers doing in schools to prepare these kids?

The messages schools put out to the greater community are very important. Communities, often charged with paying school taxes, need to see that their taxes are being used for the greater good of developing students who can be innovative. A school community with a good reputation is often the one where realtors can sell houses. How many times have you watched a real estate show or read an advertisement online that says, "great school district." People with children buy houses where there is a good school system. Community engagement matters.

Before Gavin can work with his greater community, he has some steps to take to really bring about authentic dialogue. Considering this is a coaching book, it's important that the coach help the leader work through some of these implications. Although the following examples are taken from the university level, they are completely relevant to the relationship between the K–12 school system and the community at large.

Dempsey (2010) highlighted four areas to consider when engaging with the school community. Following are those four areas, adapted for the K–12 setting:

- School participants should not expect to launch these partnerships without considering how their school is already affecting community stakeholders in both positive and negative ways.
- Community engagement efforts should take active measures to surface issues of difference between and among participants.
- School participants should take measures to anticipate and actively mitigate the ways in which community engagement efforts reproduce existing material inequalities within and between communities.
- Community engagement requires a willingness on the part of its participants to engage in the murky and contentious process of pursuing mutually transformative programs for change.

The last area highlighted by Dempsey supports research on collaboration by Kuhn (2015), who found that, "more productive collaborations have been identified as those in which participants directly engage one another's thinking. They listen and respond to what their peers say" (p. 47).

MICHELLE'S COMMUNITY ENGAGEMENT COACHING CONVERSATION

"I know that CLT was difficult, but I think there were some people who spoke up who don't usually do so. That's a major win, Gavin," Michelle says, as Gavin nods in agreement. "As you know, I like going back to our goal and current reality. What is the current reality of the CLT?" Michelle asks.

"At the beginning of the year, and even halfway through, I would have said I run the meeting and the agenda, and a few of the same people always speak up. Over the last few months, though, I will say there is a renewed excitement about CLT. We have co-chairs that are fairly confident in their roles, and we have stakeholders who have a clear understanding of their roles because we established it together and I sent out a follow up email about it," Gavin responds.

"You seem a little hesitant," Michelle says.

"I am. I think the meeting went well, and the feedback was great. However, I also know that Michael Fullan writes a lot about the implementation dip, so I'm keen to understand that yesterday was great but it was merely the beginning," Gavin says.

Michelle is impressed that Gavin doesn't just get caught up in the positive of the CLT meeting but also understands that there is still a lot of work to do even beyond this year.

"So, knowing that, what would you say is your full current reality?" Michelle asks.

Gavin realizes it was something he thought about in the back of his mind, but this was the first time he was articulating it. "I think I need to make sure that although I'm an equal member of the CLT, I have to be cognizant of the fact that there will be an implementation dip. Maybe I will even bring this up at our next meeting. However, I just feel like every time I have a focus, it opens up and is not nicely packaged," he says.

Before Michelle can ask what he means by that, Gavin continues, "Leadership is not like a drama we watch on television. It doesn't get wrapped up neatly at the end of the year like at the end of a show. It keeps going forward, and we don't always know how it will end because it never really does. We are just merely parts of the show and have to do our best with all of the twists and turns, even when we don't see them coming."

Michelle thinks that is fairly profound.

IN THE END

Gavin and Michelle's coaching relationship is almost through its first year. After establishing trust and determining where Gavin really wanted to spend his time, they established the CLT for Naylor Middle School. As most leaders know, a stakeholder group like CLT does not just get put together and jump into deep learning regarding a problem of practice for the school. It takes time and effort to build relationships where people feel as though they can have an open discussion regarding problem areas in a school building.

After fostering trust, they began to look at four priorities, which are collective efficacy, communication, student and community engagement, and the political climate, which is addressed in Chapter 10. Truthfully, this chapter may have included some of the most controversial and difficult topics to talk about as a team. Many schools have mottos that say "*All Means All*," but in reality there is often a group, or set of groups, that is not part of that "all" statement, which is why the topic of minoritized populations came up.

While we find ourselves deep into the 21st century, in discussion with leaders it becomes apparent that we still have groups that feel left out of the school community. We need not look any further than the political climate in the United States as well as other countries to see that groups do not feel included. As school leaders, we need to make sure we do a better job of fostering a school climate that is inclusive of all of those groups. If we are not doing that in our schools, then what are we doing? Every student should feel included and welcome.

The CLT is establishing collective efficacy among the group because members are challenging each other's thinking regarding a problem of practice that they together deem to be important. The positive side of all of this is that the conversations they have as a group work like grassroots efforts and make their way into conversations with their smaller department PLCs. And those same conversations regarding minoritized groups enter into discussions in classrooms and then discussions that take place at home. Make no mistake—it's not about furthering an agenda but about coming to an understanding about each other.

Last, we know Gavin is becoming a stronger leader, but even he understands that all of this learning, dialogue, and action will not end on the last day of the school year. They will cycle into the next school year as well. And that's why setting the foundation, much like the CLT did, is so vitally important.

DISCUSSION QUESTIONS

Coaches and Leaders:

- How do you feel about the way Michelle is coaching? Would that work for you?

Leaders:

- How does community engagement fit into your priorities as a principal?
- Would you have approached setting up the CLT differently than Gavin?

- How do you maintain focus when your mind begins to wander into next year and beyond?

Coaches:

- As a coach, how do you help leaders prioritize? Do those priorities fit with the priority outlined here in this chapter?
- When do you begin to back off from coaching to empower leaders after you have worked with them for a while?

TAKE ACTION

- Please address the controversial topics covered in this chapter.
- Work with outside agencies that have expertise.
- Vet their resources. Make sure they understand your current reality.

10

PRIORITY IV–THE POLITICAL CLIMATE

I was fortunate enough to be asked to provide feedback and edits on John Hattie's report (2015), *What Doesn't Work in Education: The Politics of Distraction*. It was the first time he had ever asked me to do that, and I was nervous. However, I quickly got over who I was editing and dove deep into the manuscript. Hattie began by stating that we talk too much about adult issues and not enough about learning.

We see this in virtually every aspect of education. Whether we are looking at the national state level, we spend way too much time talking about teachers, and it's usually a negative conversation.

When it comes to our own board meetings, we see board of education members who ran for election because they had one issue they wanted to address with their child's school or they were using it as a stepping stone for a political appointment. Too few times do we see board members who care about the education of all of our students. Fortunately, I have met some board members who come to my trainings, workshops, and keynotes, and that gives me hope that there are more board of education members who want to learn how to have an impact on student learning in their school districts.

As a school leader, politics can take up a great deal of our time, and Gavin is no different. In this chapter we explore how Gavin deals with the politics of distraction.

As Gavin stated earlier, there is a lot of negative rhetoric about school and education. One of the difficulties for school leaders is to keep a focus on learning when there are so many outside influences that can impact the conversations within school. Gavin and his CLT are trying to focus on learning, and they are approaching it through a concentration on academics and social–emotional learning while also trying to build collective efficacy.

Michelle understands that one of the priorities, and often the biggest obstacle, a leader can face is politics. The U.S. educational system, for example, seems to be based on a political cycle and not a pedagogical one. She knows that leaders often hear that politics are a part of their job, and that is absolutely true because it plays out at the building, district, state, and national level.

Michelle attended a national conference and went to Michael Fullan's keynote address. In his keynote, Fullan said, "Just because you're stuck with their policies doesn't mean you need to be stuck with their mindset." Michelle walked away from that moment feeling the full weight of Fullan's powerful quotation, because there were times during her leadership when she got caught up in the noise and had to step back and reflect on what she wanted out of it.

In their conversations, Michelle tells Gavin that it's easy to get caught up in the politics, especially when dealing, for example, with a board member whose sole agenda seems to be about his or her own child rather than the rest of the school community. Gavin knows this all too well. The president of the school board has a child in Gavin's school and has tried a few times to talk to Gavin as a board member concerned about issues happening at Naylor Middle School. At first Gavin was taken aback and did whatever he could to entertain the board member, but then Dr. Coppola intervened and made sure that all issues from the board go through her first. Gavin became savvy enough that he told the board president when it was time to end a conversation.

In another political realm, Gavin needs to work with Brad and Beth on state mandates and accountability measures. He understands that the national level has offered more complications than ever before because of issues like the No Child Left Behind Act, the former Race to the Top legislation, which still impacts the way teachers think, as well as the ever changing Every Student Succeeds Act (ESSA). Gavin is beginning to understand why his older administrative colleagues say that education in many countries has too long been based on a political cycle instead of a pedagogical one. He also understands that it doesn't often matter which party is in power; the politics outweigh what is good for students.

NEGATIVE RHETORIC AFFECTS US TOO

Michelle remembers a time when there was more local control over schools, and districts were left to their own devices and were somewhat shielded by state and national politics. However, after the *Nation at Risk* report in the early 1980s (The National Commission on Excellence in Education, 1983), things began to take a drastic turn, never more so than the No Child Left Behind Act in the early 2000s. Schools began seeing increased accountability requirements and an increase in the use of standardized tests from Grades 3 through 8. Over the last decade, which Gavin spent as a teacher, assistant principal, and now a principal, standardized testing has become a battleground for educators, and this has a profound effect on leaders.

Where Gavin still gets stuck is with initiatives that trickle down to the building level. One of the areas that Michelle is working on with Gavin, and Gavin is working on with Beth and Brad, is how to address these initiatives. Michelle has helped Gavin take a step back and ask the following questions:

- What are the initiatives really about?
- What are the pros and cons of those initiatives?
- Can we use them to guide learning?
- How much "control" do we have over them?
- If we don't have control, how can we let it go and get them done?

HATTIE'S POLITICS OF DISTRACTION

Michelle tells Gavin there is another side of politics, and it's something Hattie wrote about in his report (Hattie, 2015). "He has an interesting take on all of this, as you can imagine," Michelle says.

Gavin is still becoming familiar with Hattie's research, and it is quite a bit of rhetoric and research to take in.

Michelle continues, "Hattie found that those making decisions would often make them based more on politics than what the research said. This has implications not just for policy makers but also for leaders who get caught up in their politics of distraction as well."

Gavin nods his head in agreement and says, "I have to admit it's not always easy to separate the politics I have to deal with from the goals I'm working on with you."

Coach's Corner

Beware of the Politics of Distraction

In Hattie's report (2015), he divided the distractions into the following areas:

- *Distraction 1: Appease the parents—If we make the parents happy we will all be happy!*
- *Distraction 2: Fix the infrastructure—More technology will make things better!*
- *Distraction 3: Fix the students—If we only had better students!*
- *Distraction 4: Fix the schools—Our schools are not innovative and they are too far behind!*
- *Distraction 5: Fix the teachers—Teachers are lackluster. They need more training!*

Michelle smiles in agreement and responds, "Believe me, I got caught up in those things as well. I think Hattie's distractions helps us highlight some of those issues, and that makes it a little easier … not always easy, but a little easier."

Michelle begins to explain Hattie's distractions by saying, "For example, one way to appease parents is by reducing class size. Class size is one of those topics that comes up often in education debates, and we have talked about it several times in our discussions together over the last few months."

Gavin nods in agreement, remembering some of the spirited discussions he has also had with teachers.

Michelle continues, "Districts, states, and ministries of education spend a great deal of money to reduce it, but it doesn't have the high yield effect that many would like it to have. This is where educators and smaller class size advocates get angry. What Hattie said is that class size doesn't presently matter because very often teachers will not change the way they instruct students. If we want class size to matter, we have to ensure that teachers change their instructional practices in a way that will help foster more student growth, like providing increased feedback, increasing student talk in the classroom, and including more authentic, collaborative working time among students."

Michelle explains that instead of ignoring the politics, it's important that leaders understand their current reality. Over the time they have been working together, Michelle has helped Gavin deliver a mandate without using bias so he can bring it objectively to staff and therefore ask them to work collaboratively in a way that will still allow them to feel that they have a voice in the process even though the mandate came from the top.

Other times Michelle has helped provide perspective to Gavin. They have worked collaboratively to brainstorm ways to alleviate the tension that comes along with politics. Michelle has helped Gavin keep a laser-like focus on what would constitute the best learning experiences for students so they can exceed their own potential.

THE COLLABORATIVE LEADERSHIP TEAM
GETS DISTRACTED

Winter is long over and Naylor Middle School finds itself deep into spring. Although it seems like an exciting time for schools because summer is quickly approaching and students are moving on to the high school soon, it is also a highly stressful time because of candidates running for the school board and the school budget being put to a vote by the community. The budget vote in Naylor is always worrisome because a small increase in the school budget will fall on the backs of taxpayers, and there is no shortage of community members and parents who post on social media that teachers and administrators make too much money and that the community cannot afford to keep paying more and more.

Gavin has taken a break from social media, but Beth and a few teachers have not. What they read every night and in the early morning as they drink their coffee comes in with them when they enter school. "It's hard when we work so hard and the community doesn't support us," Beth confides to Gavin one morning as she is getting ready for the day.

"Actually, the majority of the community does support us," Gavin reminds her.

"Well, the majority is pretty quiet these days," Beth responds.

"Maybe we need to find a way to inspire them to speak up a bit more," Gavin says.

Beth stands silently, reflecting for a moment. She knows that getting the silent majority to speak up means that they, as a leadership team, have to look at how they listen to the community during the good times and bad. Maybe there is a reason for the silent majority.

After Beth leaves his office, Gavin checks Twitter to see if he has missed anything important from his social media PLN. He sees numerous tweets in response to the last tweet from the president, and then he notices one from his Twitter friend Kara Vandas. Kara asked her son what he wanted out of a principal, and he wrote a list that she tweeted and many others retweeted.

It was the quick jolt that Gavin needed to move on through his day. "Thanks, Myer," he thought to himself.

At the CLT meeting, Gavin expects, and is right in his expectation, that this will come up. "Why are we doing so much extra when the community doesn't care?" Janelle asks.

"Because we're doing it for the kids," Gavin responds.

"I have to be honest that I really don't like that statement," Anika says, looking at Gavin. "Every time we have a real concern about our community support or lack thereof, someone always says we are doing it for the kids. We know that already."

Gavin's face turns red. He wanted teacher voice and now he has it.

"Listen. I get that you are angry," Brad says, and Gavin is really happy that he is speaking out. "But I don't think we have to be rude either. Gavin is right that we have to step back and think about how this CLT process should focus on student learning," Brad continues.

"I'm sorry Gavin. I didn't mean to be rude. It's just that some of the parents have been really negative on social media," Anika says.

"Well, it doesn't mean we have to be negative too," Gavin responds.

Anika looks down at her laptop.

"We get caught up in the noise and spend too much time focusing on the things we don't control. As a CLT we have spent a lot of time on our communication, and families have responded well, right?" Gavin asks.

A majority of the group nod their heads in agreement.

"The people on social media who are being negative—Are they our families?" Gavin asks.

"No," Cherise and Brian answer together. "They are from the high school."

"So maybe, just maybe, we don't have the issues we think we do. Perhaps our families do support us," Gavin continues.

Over the 90 minutes of their meeting, Gavin brings them back to their original goals of collective efficacy, which they have established over the year, and then they focus on communication, engagement, inclusiveness, and equity.

Over the year, Gavin has flipped his communication practices to allow families to get some surface-level information before PTA meetings, Open House, and parent–teacher conferences. The school sends home a one-page newsletter per month. The leaders, as well as many of the teachers, struggle with communicating too much and then with communicating too little. The CLT began discussing the Goldilocks principle where communication is concerned, so they asked families how often they want communication from the main office, as opposed to how often they want communication from teachers. CLT sent surveys to families looking for guidance. Many of the respondents said that once a week was sufficient when it came to communication from both teachers and the main office, because sometimes it was overwhelming. Gavin and the rest of the CLT decided that updating the school website would be a great way to keep families informed as well. This, of course, is in addition to the normal day-to-day communication Gavin, the assistant principals, and teachers have with families, when they are dropping off their children or when there is a certain need to be addressed.

This helped greatly with the politics of distraction, because out in the community there was a buzz around the fact that the school seemed to be listening to the needs of families. That buzz certainly helped during times like budget votes and board meetings.

Within the school, Gavin and his assistant principals send out a Friday morning message with important information, which includes a teacher voice section. They found that not all teachers were reading the messages, so they sent staff a survey asking how often, and in what forms, they wanted main office communication. Once a week was what most of them said. This time, approximately 80% of staff answered the survey, which is an increase in participation from the last time Gavin offered a survey to staff.

They have seen their department-level PLCs become stronger, with a focus on student learning and gathering of evidence based on Donohoo's (Donohoo & Velasco, 2016) collaborative inquiry model. And last but not least, they explored more inclusive topics by creating a Gay–Straight Alliance in their school as well as opening up some gender-neutral bathrooms. Yes, Gavin agrees that it came with some pushback from parents, but a lot of that has been alleviated over time. As they sit and talk, they realize that their CLT has accomplished a lot over the year, and for about 80 of the 90 minutes, they forget about the politics of distraction.

"We have to do more of this," Gavin says. "We have to celebrate our successes more than we normally do. I mean, look around this library. We have sections focusing on equity and minoritized populations. Our hallways have amazing student art hanging up, and the new mural that Beth and Ann Marie painted in the hallway is exactly what we set out to do when we wanted our student population represented in our pictures. Let's not lose sight of the fact that we have created a more inclusive school climate, and it's beginning to change our culture."

The CLT can't argue with the work that has been done. Although team members have more to do, they came together as a group, challenged each other's thinking, and had an impact on the school community. Sure, there are still some teachers who are naysayers, but overall, the teachers and support staff are much more engaged.

IN THE END

Leadership is not for the faint of heart. Every day leaders are bombarded with questions, criticisms, and feedback. It's hard for leaders to be proactive when they enter into the building every day with their heads down waiting for the next shoe to drop, awaiting battle. Other times leadership is much more gratifying. Leaders will hear praise from parents and teachers, or better yet, have great conversations with students in the hallway where they feel like they're creating relationships with different stakeholders and moving their building climate in a much more positive direction.

What makes building leadership even more complicated is this idea of self-efficacy on the part of each staff member and how to help build collective efficacy among staff in a building. Self-efficacy and collective efficacy need to be a cornerstone of our thinking because not only do they play an important role in a school climate but also in the success of our students, and this is the reason why collective efficacy is one of the priorities we focused on as well.

In this chapter, Michelle and Gavin focused on the politics of distraction that can get in the way of doing the quality work they originally wanted to do. We saw how Gavin had to help members of the CLT refocus their efforts on their original goals.

High-quality coaches, like Michelle, help leaders understand their current reality in relation to these priorities to get a better sense of where they need to start. As time goes on, Gavin will continue to get stronger at helping Brad and Beth do the same thing. It's important that a coach and leader discuss the current reality and get a sense of different options before they move on. Ultimately, it is our hope that leaders and coaches will start small and work on one priority that will help them grow.

DISCUSSION QUESTIONS

- How can leaders and coaches work together to focus on the collective efficacy of teachers?
- How do the politics of distraction work as both a priority and an obstacle for leaders?
- Out of the four priorities established in this chapter, which one is of the greatest value for you as a leader?
- What one goal could you choose that might help you address the four priorities at the same time?
- Understanding the priorities, why is it important that leaders work with a coach who truly understands their needs?

TAKE ACTION

Look at your school climate. Does it have the following enabling conditions?

- Board policies and student codes of conduct that are inclusive of all minoritized populations
- Images in hallways that represent all students
- Inclusive curriculum
- Inclusive books and novels that represent minoritized populations positively
- Common language around learning
- Partnerships with outside agencies that understand your context

Epilogue

Where Does Gavin Go From Here?

When we look at leadership coaching, we often make the mistake of thinking it's about one person and one goal, but that's just one piece of a much larger puzzle. Michelle had to introduce herself to Gavin and then prove her credibility because he initially didn't want to be coached. However, coaching Gavin involved much more than just him, because when he created the goal, it opened up a steady stream of events. One person's goal always involves more than one person if it's going to be successful, which is why you learned more about Brad, Beth, Brian, Janelle, Michelle, and Anika. It is not just the goal leaders like Gavin we have to worry about, but the reaction of others to that goal, because that will determine their level of investment.

///

Brian's Story

Brian Bellagio has been teaching social studies at Naylor Middle School for five years. Before that he taught for six years at a high-poverty city school in the area. The only reason he left that school and moved to Naylor was that he was offered an opportunity to direct plays for the after-school drama program besides teaching social studies. Drama was his minor in college, so he was excited.

It's not that he minded Alan as a school principal, but he found that he couldn't talk about the topics he wanted to discuss because he lacked administrative support. One time he delved into talking about transgender students because students came in asking questions. The night before there was a story about transgender students all over the local and national news. Brian always believed part of his job was to teach about topics that come up in society, in a way that students understand. Unfortunately, two students went home and told their parents about the discussion, which resulted in two parents calling Alan the next day, and Brian was told that he should stick to the curriculum and ask for permission before discussing such topics.

Brian was conflicted because he knew that LGBTQ discussions were a part of the inclusive curriculum adopted by the state, and it was supposed to be mandated, but without administrative support, Brian was not going to talk outside the line that Alan had drawn in the sand. Brian was concerned that Gavin was the same type of unsupportive administrator.

However, the discussion of minoritized populations at CLT meetings and the faculty meeting helped Brian see that Gavin is more supportive and inclusive. Brian is ready to move forward and have a discussion with the local LGBTQ community center so that it can help with additional resources, as well as provide talking points for teachers. But he also knows that not all teachers are comfortable with the topic, and they are not looking to move forward as quickly, so he wants to take on the responsibility of bringing in inclusive topics.

After the last CLT meeting, Gavin found Brian in the hallway and asked if they could talk. Brian felt a wave of disappointment come over him because he thought Gavin was going to tell him to back off from addressing any controversial topic. He was pleasantly surprised when Gavin did the opposite.

"Listen, I heard that you have not been supported in the past," Gavin began. "I want you to move forward with teaching what you see fit, especially if it's in the news and kids are talking about it. I just want a bit of a heads up in case parents will call," he explained.

"Fair enough," Brian responded.

"I'm glad we talked about it briefly at the faculty meeting and dug down deeper at the CLT, but I want to go further with this because I want all of our students to feel accepted, not tolerated," Gavin said with a smile.

Brian thanked him for the conversation.

"I know we have a long way to go, but I'm hoping you can help bring us along," Gavin said, walking away.

Brian now knows he has administrative support, and that makes a difference regardless of what topic teachers cover.

//

Over the time Gavin worked with Michelle, his self-efficacy as a leader increased because he felt confident that he was working on the right goal. Make no mistake, it was his goal with Michelle, but it led to more collaboration among staff, which makes his goal the catalyst in benefiting the great good of the school community.

It took about a month of weekly meetings for Gavin to really trust Michelle, but as you read through each chapter, you could see the trust grow, and Michelle began to find a balance with how often they met in person. After about two months, their face-to-face meetings took place every other week.

Gavin's ultimate goal was to create a CLT, and through that process individuals found their voice. Fostering teacher leadership is one of Donohoo's (2017) enabling conditions. Fostering teacher leadership is important because too often schools have one teacher leader, when in reality they need more than that because not every teacher connects with the chosen teacher leader. Fostering teacher leadership out of a variety of teachers also sends an important message to staff that they all bring a level of expertise to the profession. We need to spread the wealth and foster climates that show how great our teachers really are. The negative rhetoric about teaching and teachers has been too widespread, and collaboration and teacher leadership can help negate and combat it.

As Gavin walked around the hallways and had conversations with different teachers, assistants, and specialists over the months he worked with Michelle, he noticed that staff began to share a common language about learning. What this meant to Gavin was that those hours at faculty meetings where they talked about the true definition of student engagement, scaffolding, minoritized populations, and communication led to transfer learning where teachers and staff were using those definitions in their daily conversations. Gavin, Beth, and Brad also made a conscious effort to get people to stop using so many educational acronyms with families, so that they feel less confused and more included when talking to teachers and leaders in the school.

From a distance, Dr. Coppola watched Gavin's progress. She didn't need Michelle to bend her ear and tell her all of the details, because she talked to Gavin from time to time to ask how it was going, and she saw a difference in the way he led the building, as well as the growth of the CLT. We need to remember that Gavin heard stories of how the building was when Alan was there, but Dr. Coppola is the superintendent and she lived it. She had consistent interactions with Alan and saw how he interacted with the school community, and Dr. Coppola could see a change in the building culture over the year that Gavin was being coached.

Truthfully, however, they still have a long way to go until all teachers and staff share in that common language of learning. Additionally, they need to foster that same common language among families, all of which we are confident that Gavin can achieve through the hard work of the staff at Naylor Middle School.

UNDERSTANDING PRIORITIES

Over the next year, Michelle and Gavin would continue to meet monthly. As much as the CLT had a focus, there were new initiatives that came into the district that took their focus off learning strategies and common language around what makes a good learner. They made a conscious effort to regroup and come back to their core mission as a CLT, which was to focus on student learning.

When it came to exploring minoritized populations, the CLT brought in an expert from a local community group, which Brian and Dr. Coppola found for them, and that expert joined the last faculty meeting. Teachers, specialists, and staff learned about a common language to use around their LGBTQ population. The person was engaging, and more importantly, he understood the context of Naylor Middle School because he had several phone calls with Gavin and even sent out a preengagement survey to staff to gather more information about how the staff felt. The faculty decided they wanted one more presentation from the community center in the new year before they held discussions with students and included new inclusive books and curriculum. Truthfully, many of the staff members didn't yet have a sense of self-efficacy when it came to including inclusive topics.

FOUR PRIORITIES

Keeping in mind the four priorities of a leader, Gavin, Michelle, Beth, Brad, and the rest of the CLT had to constantly question how they were communicating to staff, students, and parents. They did their best to always come back to their moral purpose, which was to focus on engaging more and more students with authentic learning experiences. Some teachers were resistant and were negative at meetings, but most of the staff continued to maintain their focus while also trying to sway resistant staff.

Gavin knew that those teachers who showed student growth in their classroom were afforded more autonomy than those who were resistant and didn't show student growth. More so, Gavin took steps to put several teachers on performance plans over his first few years. This is something that Michelle helped him with as well, because she had experience in that area.

Additionally, each time CLT members had a conversation about their moral purpose, Gavin would pull out a letter written by a student. At the last meeting, he displayed a letter written by Tevyn Owira. Gavin had asked a group of students what they wanted out of their principal for the next year, now that they had gotten to know him as their principal this year. Tevyn provided some very good advice and wrote in simple terms about what principals should and shouldn't do and offered some helpful advice on how they should act.

What Principals Should Do:

One thing a principal should do is try to learn every students' name in the school, whether they are a well-behaved student or not. The principal should stop in to classrooms randomly to see what they are learning and doing in class. A principal should schedule events within the school, even after school, to encourage kids to enjoy school. This should especially occur around times of state testing or other difficult exams, so students don't think of school just as a negative place but a place you can have fun and enjoy too.

What Principals Shouldn't Do:

One thing a principal should not do is be disrespectful to students or staff members, especially in front of other people. A principal should not be late to school. If a principal makes a commitment to participate in an event, he or she should not back out of that commitment. I believe a principal should take bullying incidents very seriously and not sweep it under the rug.

How Principals Should Act:

A principal should be funny and have a sense of humor, but in more important cases, I understand a principal should be serious. I think that he or she should remain calm in those cases as well.

Tevyn
Sixth Grade

Gavin found the letters so profound, he would often begin each CLT meeting with a different stakeholder reading one. It reminded them of why they were there.

In the End

In this story, which I used to highlight the coaching process between a coach and a leader, I tried my best to show the growing trust among all the characters but also the idea that coaching is about asking good questions, and leadership is about reflecting with evidence and engaging as many stakeholders as possible.

Whatever road leaders take, I hope that the focus is always on student learning. We need great leaders who understand the impact of social–emotional, as well as academic, learning, and it starts by having people around who will help challenge leaders enough so that they grow.

DISCUSSION QUESTIONS

- Would you work with a leadership coach? Why or why not?
- If you decided to work with a coach, what would you want out of that relationship?
- What could a coach help you learn that you may be unable to learn on your own or with staff?
- Have you ever had an experience like Gavin's? What did you learn from it?
- What kind of leader do you want to be?

Afterword

The educational shift in the past two decades has high-lighted the importance of leadership development for school leaders. The days of principals being only the manager of the building are gone. The increased job responsibilities of a manager AND instructional leader highlight the importance of providing purposeful coaching to young school leaders. As a result, the Oklahoma State Department of Education, in partnership with South Central Comprehensive Center and EDUTAS at The University of Oklahoma, developed a professional learning program for assistant principals and new head principals—Moving UP: Transitioning into the Principalship. The program focus is to build leaders' skills and competencies by filling their toolboxes with practical, job-embedded strategies.

After the first pilot year, the partners further refined the knowledge and practice areas most needed and requested by early career Oklahoma administrators. We found that Peter DeWitt's work on collaborative leadership and school climate aligned perfectly with our greatest needs and highest priorities, so we engaged him for our second full cohort.

Throughout the five-session series with Peter, our principals spent time learning, reflecting, practicing, and then documenting their personal and professional growth around instructional leadership, collective efficacy, professional learning and development, assessment-capable learners, feedback, and family engagement—six of John Hattie's influences that

Peter presented in depth to support the participants' roles as instructional leaders and communicators.

In keeping with the dynamic coaching relationship and principles laid out in *Coach It Further* and established for Moving UP, Peter carefully listened, then adjusted content, conversations, and strategies to best accommodate the learners' needs within their local context. After each session the partners, coaches, and Peter debriefed and reviewed participant feedback to personalize follow-up coaching and differentiate content for the next session. He modeled *Coach It Further* before he wrote this book!

Throughout our engagement with Peter, the Moving UP partners worked in a very close coaching relationship with him, as did the executive coaches we provided for the pilot principals. With the benefit of multiple layers of coaching and knowledge, skill and trust-building exercises, our principal participants are now better prepared to serve as the collaborative leaders and instructional coaches in their building, and their schools and students will be better for it.

Time and again our school leaders remarked about the unique opportunity to work directly with Peter because of his authenticity and credibility. Similarly, the Moving UP coaching and conversation components they valued the most were live scenarios, much like those in *Coach it Further.* In his role as a coach, Peter helped build participants' self-efficacy and confidence to move ahead with coaching others at their schools.

I valued the "ability to see a need and develop a plan beyond the scope of normal AP responsibilities," one participant remarked, while another said, "I am forever changed." As to the impact of having a coach "during this stressful year of transitioning into a new position[, it] was an absolute blessing! I'm confident my learning here is affecting my staff. Specifically, the formal and informal feedback I [can now] provide to my staff," another said.

While Peter is already a best-selling author, it was very clear to us that he is also a pragmatic, efficacious leader and coach who drives for results and gets them. An early lesson for all of us involved with Moving UP was how essential the learning, support, and coaching is for assistant principals and how little is readily available.

Our work with Peter, and his with us, confirmed and heightened our shared commitment to an ongoing learning and development process in support of emerging leaders. Peter carefully wove theory into the practical work with our principals with humor and humility. As a result, we grew. We look forward to our next engagement with Peter and trust that this book, like his others, will strike a chord with its readers as authentic, personal, and doable. Thanks Peter for coaching it further in Oklahoma.

Robin Anderson, Oklahoma State Department of Education

Lisa Pryor, EDUTAS at The University of Oklahoma

References

Bandura, A. (1977). Self-efficacy: Toward a unifying theory of behavioral change. *Psychological Review, 84*(2), 191–215.

Bandura, A. (1997). *Self-efficacy: The exercise of control.* New York: W. H. Freeman.

Bryk, A. S., & Schneider, B. (2003). Trust in schools: A core resource for school reform. *Educational Leadership, 60*(6), 40–45.

Covey, S. R. (1990). *The 7 habits of highly effective people.* New York, NY: Free Press.

Dempsey, S. E. (2010). Critiquing community engagement. *Management Communication Quarterly, 24*(3), 359–390.

DeWitt, P. (2016, October 16). If coaching is so powerful, why aren't principals being coached? *Education Week.* Retrieved from http://blogs.edweek.org/edweek/finding_common_ground/2016/10/if_coaching_is_so_powerful_why_aren't_principals_being_coached.html

Donohoo, J. (2017). *Collective efficacy: How educators' beliefs impact student learning.* Thousand Oaks, CA: Corwin.

Donohoo, J., & Velasco, M. (2016). *The transformative power of collaborative inquiry: Realizing change in schools and classrooms.* Thousand Oaks, CA: Corwin.

Doran, G. T. (1981). There's a S.M.A.R.T. way to write management's goals and objectives. Retrieved from https://community.mis.temple.edu/mis0855002fall2015/files/2015/10/S.M.A.R.T-Way-Management-Review.pdf

Harper, S. R. (2012). Race without racism: How higher education researchers minimize racist institutional norms [Supplement]. *The Review of Higher Education, 36*(1), 9–29.

Hattie, J. (2012a). *Visible learning for teachers: Maximizing impact on learning.* London, UK: Routledge.

Hattie, J. (2012b). Know thy impact. *Educational Leadership, 70*(1), 18–23.

Hattie, J. (2015). *What doesn't work in education: The politics of distraction.* London, UK: Pearson.

Knight, J. (2007). *Instructional coaching: A partnership approach to improving instruction.* Thousand Oaks, CA: Corwin.

Knight, J. (2011). *Unmistakable impact. A partnership approach for dramatically improving instruction.* Thousand Oaks, CA: Corwin.

Kuhn, D. (2015). Thinking together and alone. *Educational Researcher, 44*(1), 46–53.

Leithwood, K., & Jantzi, D. (2008). Linking leadership to student learning: The contributions of leader efficacy. *Educational Administration Quarterly, 44*(4), 496–528.

Lencioni, P. M. (2005). *Overcoming the five dysfunctions of a team.* Hoboken, NJ: John Wiley & Sons.

Pink, D. H. (2018, February 16). How to be healthier, happier and more productive: It's all in the timing. *The Wall Street Journal.* Retrieved from https://www.wsj.com/articles/how-to-be-healthier-happier-and-more-productive-its-all-in-the-timing-1514560647

Pont, B., Nusche, D., & Moorman, H. (2008). *Improving school leadership: Volume 1: Policy and practice.* Paris, France: Organisation for Economic Co-Operation and Development.

Quaglia, R., & Lande, L. (2014). *Teacher voice report 2010–2014.* Portland, ME: Quaglia Institute.

Robinson, V. (2011). *Student-centered leadership.* San Francisco, CA: Jossey-Bass.

Ruben, B. D., & Gigliotti, R. A. (2016). Leadership as social influence: An expanded view of leadership communication theory and practice. *Journal of Leadership & Organizational Studies, 23*(4), 361–373.

Stone, D., & Heen, S. (2015). *Thanks for the feedback. The science and art of receiving feedback well.* London, UK: Penguin Books.

The National Commission on Excellence in Education. (1983, April). *A nation at risk: The imperative for educational reform.* Washington, DC: U.S. Government Printing Office.

Tschannen-Moran, M., & Gareis, C. R. (2004). Principals' sense of efficacy: Assessing a promising construct. *Journal of Educational Administration, 42*(5), 575–585.

Witherspoon, R. (2014). Double-loop coaching for leadership development. *The Journal of Applied Behavioral Science, 50*(3), 261–283.

CORWIN LEADERSHIP

Anthony Kim & Alexis Gonzales-Black

Designed to foster flexibility and continuous innovation, this resource expands cutting-edge management and organizational techniques to empower schools with the agility and responsiveness vital to their new environment.

Jonathan Eckert

Explore the collective and reflective approach to progress, process, and programs that will build conditions that lead to strong leadership and teaching, which will improve student outcomes.

PJ Caposey

Offering a fresh perspective on teacher evaluation, this book guides administrators to transform their school culture and evaluation process to improve teacher practice and, ultimately, student achievement.

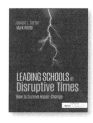

Dwight L. Carter & Mark White

Through understanding the past and envisioning the future, the authors use practical exercises and real-life examples to draw the blueprint for adapting schools to the age of hyper-change.

Raymond L. Smith & Julie R. Smith

This solid, sustainable, and laser-sharp focus on instructional leadership strategies for coaching might just be your most impactful investment toward student achievement.

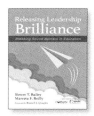

Simon T. Bailey & Marceta F. Reilly

This engaging resource provides a simple, sustainable framework that will help you move your school from mediocrity to brilliance.

Debbie Silver & Dedra Stafford

Equip educators to develop resilient and mindful learners primed for academic growth and personal success.

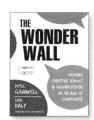

Peter Gamwell & Jane Daly

Discover a new perspective on how to nurture creativity, innovation, leadership, and engagement.

Leadership That Makes an Impact

Steven Katz, Lisa Ain Dack, & John Malloy
Leverage the oppositional forces of top-down expectations and bottom-up experience to create an intelligent, responsive school.

Peter M. DeWitt
Centered on staff efficacy, these resources present discussion questions, vignettes, strategies, and action steps to improve school climate, leadership collaboration, and student growth.

Eric Sheninger
Harness digital resources to create a new school culture, increase communication and student engagement, facilitate real-time professional growth, and access new opportunities for your school.

Russell J. Quaglia, Kristine Fox, Deborah Young, Michael J. Corso, & Lisa L. Lande
Listen to your school's voice to see how you can increase engagement, involvement, and academic motivation.

Michael Fullan, Joanne Quinn, & Joanne McEachen
Learn the right drivers to mobilize complex, coherent, whole-system change and transform learning for all students.

CORWIN LEADERSHIP

A SAGE Publishing Company

CORWIN HAS ONE MISSION: to enhance education through intentional professional learning.

We build long-term relationships with our authors, educators, clients, and associations who partner with us to develop and continuously improve the best evidence-based practices that establish and support lifelong learning.